Web 2.0: Making the Web Work for You

ILLUSTRATED

Web 2.0: Making the Web Work for You

ILLUSTRATED

Jane Hosie-Bounar/Barbara M. Waxer

COURSE TECHNOLOGY
CENGAGE Learning

Australia • Brazil • Japan • Korea • Mexico • Singapore • Spain • United Kingdom • United States

Web 2.0: Making the Web Work for You—Illustrated
Jane Hosie-Bounar/Barbara M. Waxer

Executive Editor: Marjorie Hunt

Associate Acquisitions Editor: Brandi Shailer

Senior Product Manager: Christina Kling Garrett

Associate Product Manager: Michelle Camisa

Editorial Assistant: Kim Klasner

Director of Marketing: Cheryl Costantini

Senior Marketing Manager: Ryan DeGrote

Marketing Coordinator: Kristen Panciocco

Developmental Editors: Barbara Waxer, Jane Hosie-Bounar

Content Project Manager: Lisa Weidenfeld

Copy Editor: Camille Kiolbasa

Proofreader: Chris Clark

Indexer: Rich Carlson

QA Manuscript Reviewers: John Frietas, Marianne Snow, Jeff Schwartz

Permission Specialist: Kathleen Ryan

Cover Designer: GEX Publishing Services

Cover Artist: Mark Hunt

Composition: GEX Publishing Services

© 2011 Course Technology, Cengage Learning

ALL RIGHTS RESERVED. No part of this work covered by the copyright herein may be reproduced, transmitted, stored or used in any form or by any means graphic, electronic, or mechanical, including but not limited to photocopying, recording, scanning, digitizing, taping, Web distribution, information networks, or information storage and retrieval systems, except as permitted under Section 107 or 108 of the 1976 United States Copyright Act, without the prior written permission of the publisher.

For product information and technology assistance, contact us at
Cengage Learning Customer & Sales Support, 1-800-354-9706

For permission to use material from this text or product, submit all requests online at **cengage.com/permissions**
Further permissions questions can be emailed to
permissionrequest@cengage.com

Library of Congress Control Number: 2009943350

ISBN-13: 978-0-538-47321-7
ISBN-10: 0-538-47321-5

Course Technology
20 Channel Center Street
Boston, Massachusetts 02210
USA

Trademarks:
Some of the product names and company names used in this book have been used for identification purposes only and may be trademarks or registered trademarks of their respective manufacturers and sellers.

Cengage Learning is a leading provider of customized learning solutions with office locations around the globe, including Singapore, the United Kingdom, Australia, Mexico, Brazil, and Japan. Locate your local office at:
www.cengage.com/global

Cengage Learning products are represented in Canada by Nelson Education, Ltd.

To learn more about Course Technology, visit **www.cengage.com/coursetechnology**

To learn more about Cengage Learning, visit **www.cengage.com**

Purchase any of our products at your local college store or at our preferred online store **www.CengageBrain.com**

Printed in the United States of America
1 2 3 4 5 6 15 14 13 12 11 10

Brief Contents

Preface viii

Web 2.0

Unit A: Research 2.0 1
Unit B: Finding Media for Projects 23
Unit C: Collaborating and Sharing Information...47
Unit D: Perfecting Your Online Persona 67

Glossary ....Glossary 87
Index..Index 91

Contents

Preface viii

Web 2.0

Unit A: Research 2.0 1

Understanding Web 2.0 2
    A word about privacy
Understanding Research Tools 4
Finding the Best Sources 6
    When books are best
Finding Primary Sources 8
Judging a Source's Validity 10
Bookmarking and Highlighting 12
Taking Notes and Getting Organized 14
    Dealing with writer's block
Citing Sources and Creating a Bibliography 16
    A word about plagiarism
Practice 18

Unit B: Finding Media for Projects 23

Understanding Copyright 24
    Understanding copyright infringement and the public domain
Using Creative Commons 26
Finding Images 28
Finding Video 30
    Understanding the right of publicity and right of privacy
Finding Music 32
    Creating music collaboratively online
Obtaining Permission and Crediting Sources 34
Understanding Terms of Use 36
Posting Your Files Online 38
    Fair use examples
Protecting the Rights to Your Work 40
Practice 42

Unit C: Collaborating and Sharing Information 47
Viewing Government Web Sites 48
Understanding Business and Web 2.0 50
Scheduling Meetings 52
Brainstorming Solutions 54
Using Online Polling 56
    Understanding push polls
Using Collaborative Software 58
    Doing business and governing from the clouds
Presenting Your Work 60
    Understanding presentation tools of the future
Practice 62

Unit D: Perfecting Your Online Persona 67
Creating Your Virtual Self 68
Ensuring Privacy 70
Understanding How the Virtual World Sees You 72
    A warning about posting photos and videos
Understanding Professional Networking 74
Choosing Professional Organizations 76
Working with Blogs and Microblogs 78
    Making your blog work for you
Managing Your E-Portfolio 80
    Cyberstalking
Practice 82

Glossary .... Glossary 87
Index .... Index 91

Preface

Welcome to *Web 2.0: Making the Web Work for You—Illustrated*. If this is your first experience with the Illustrated series, you'll see that this book has a unique design: each skill is presented on two facing pages, with steps on the left and screens on the right. The layout makes it easy to learn a skill without having to read a lot of text and flip pages to see an illustration.

This book is an ideal learning tool for a wide range of learners—the "rookies" will find the clean design easy to follow and focused with only essential information presented, and the "hotshots" will appreciate being able to move quickly through the lessons to find the information they need without reading a lot of text. The design also makes this a great reference after the course is over! See the illustration on the right to learn more about the pedagogical and design elements of a typical lesson.

Coverage

The latest version of the Web, called Web 2.0, is becoming an integral part of online life, from the board room to the classroom. This book will help you navigate the Web and master the tools that can get you started or move you forward. You'll learn how to research a topic and uncover primary sources; how to find and post media and understand copyright; how to collaborate online to create group projects and presentations; and how to create an effective online persona that will help you get into college, land your first job, or establish your professional or creative presence.

Each two-page spread focuses on a single skill.

Introduction briefly explains why the lesson skill is important.

A case scenario motivates the steps and puts learning in context.

Tips and troubleshooting advice, right where you need them—next to the step itself.

Large screen shots keep students on track as they complete steps

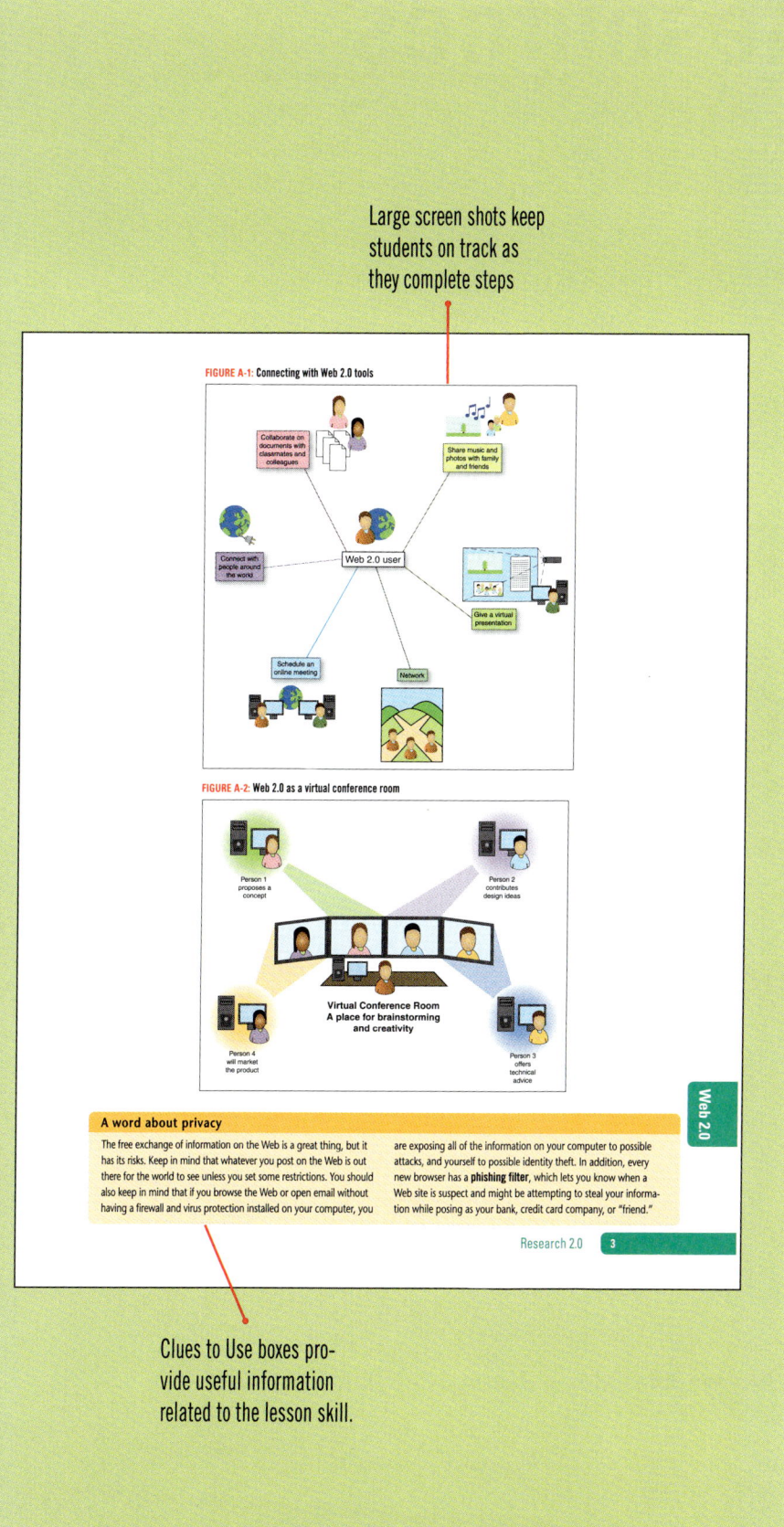

Clues to Use boxes provide useful information related to the lesson skill.

Assignments

The lessons use a realistic classroom scenario as the case study. The assignments on the yellow pages at the end of each unit increase in difficulty. Case studies provide a variety of interesting and relevant business applications. Assignments include:

- **Unit Review** consists of short answer and multiple choice questions.
- **Independent Challenges** are case projects requiring critical thinking and application of the unit skills. The Independent Challenges increase in difficulty, with the first one in each unit being the easiest. Independent Challenges 2 and 3 become increasingly open-ended, requiring more independent problem solving.
- **Visual Workshops** are practical, self-graded capstone projects that require independent problem solving.

Instructor Resources

The Instructor Resources CD is Course Technology's way of putting the resources and information needed to teach and learn effectively into your hands. With an integrated array of teaching and learning tools that offer you and your students a broad range of technology-based instructional options, we believe this CD represents the highest quality and most cutting edge resources available to instructors today. The resources available with this book are:

- **Instructor's Manual**—Available as an electronic file, the Instructor's Manual includes detailed lecture topics with teaching tips for each unit.

- **Sample Syllabus**—Prepare and customize your course easily using this sample course outline.

- **PowerPoint Presentations**—Each unit has a corresponding PowerPoint presentation that you can use in lecture, distribute to your students, or customize to suit your course.

- **Figure Files**—The figures in the text are provided on the Instructor Resources CD to help you illustrate key topics or concepts. You can create traditional overhead transparencies by printing the figure files. Or you can create electronic slide shows by using the figures in a presentation program such as PowerPoint.

- **Solutions to Exercises**—Solutions to Exercises contains examples of the work in the end-of-unit material.

- **ExamView**—ExamView is a powerful testing software package that allows you to create and administer printed, computer (LAN-based), and Internet exams. ExamView includes hundreds of questions that correspond to the topics covered in this text, enabling students to generate detailed study guides that include page references for further review. The computer-based and Internet testing components allow students to take exams at their computers, and also saves you time by grading each exam automatically.

COURSECASTS Learning on the Go. Always Available...Always Relevant.

Our fast-paced world is driven by technology. You know because you are an active participant—always on the go, always keeping up with technological trends, and always learning new ways to embrace technology to power your life. Let CourseCasts, hosted by Ken Baldauf of Florida State University, be your guide into weekly updates in this ever-changing space. These timely, relevant podcasts are produced weekly and are available for download at http://coursecasts.course.com or directly from iTunes (search by CourseCasts). CourseCasts are a perfect solution to getting students (and even instructors) to learn on the go!

Credits

Unit A

Figure A-3, Courtesy of © 2009 Google

Figure A-4, Courtesy of © 2009 University of Delaware Library

Figure A-6, Courtesy of Library of Congress

Figure A-7, Wikipedia® is a registered trademark of the Wikimedia Foundation, Inc.

Figure A-8, Courtesy of Library of Congress

Figure A-9, Courtesy of © 2009 Google

Figure A-10, Courtesy of NASA.gov

Figure A-11, Courtesy of © 2009 Google

Figure A-12, Courtesy of FBI.gov is an official site of the U.S. Federal Government, U.S. Department of Justice

Figure A-15, Courtesy of OttoBib.com

Figure A-16, Courtesy of Bibme, LLC. © 2007-2009

Figure A-17, Courtesy of Emergence of Advertising in America digital collection home page, John W. Hartman Center for Sales, Advertising & Marketing History Duke University Rare Book, Manuscript, and Special Collections Library. http://library.duke.edu/digitalcollections/eaa/

Unit B

Figure B-1, Courtesy of U.S. Copyright Office

Figures B-2, B-3, B-4, Courtesy of Creative Commons (www.creativecommons.org)

Figures B-5, B-6, B-7, Reproduced with permission of Yahoo! Inc. © 2009 Yahoo! Inc. FLICKR and the FLICKR logo are registered trademarks of Yahoo! Inc.

Figures B-8, B-9, B-10, Courtesy of Internet Archive (www.archive.org)

Figure B-11, Courtesy of Creative Commons (www.creativecommons.org)

Figures B-12, B-13, B-14, Courtesy of jamendo.com

Figure B-17, Reproduced with permission of Yahoo! Inc. © 2009 Yahoo! Inc. FLICKR and the FLICKR logo are registered trademarks of Yahoo! Inc.

Figure B-18, Courtesy of jamendo.com

Figure B-19, Courtesy of U.S. Copyright Office

Figure B-20, Courtesy of Barbara M. Waxer

Figure B-21, Courtesy of freesound.org

Figure B-22, Courtesy of Internet Archive (www.archive.org)

Unit C

Figure C-1a, Courtesy of whitehouse.gov

Figure C-1b, Courtesy of Copyright 2002–2009 Montgomery County Government All Rights Reserved

Figure C-2, Office of the Prime Minister. Reproduced with the permission of the Minister of Public Works and Government Services, 2009, and Courtesy of the Privy Council Office

Figures C-3a, C-3b, Courtesy of NASA.gov

Figure C-4, Courtesy of Cengage Learning

Figure C-5b Courtesy of FBI.gov is an official site of the U.S. Federal Government, U.S. Department of Justice

Figure C-6, Courtesy of © 2009 BackType, Inc. All Rights Reserved

Figure C-7, Courtesy of © Doodle AG

Figure C-9, Courtesy of bubbl.us

Figure C-10a, Courtesy of Facebook, © 2009

Figure C-10b, Courtesy of © BrainReactions Some rights reserved

Figures C-11a, C-11b, C-12 Courtesy of polleverywhere.com

Figure C-13a Courtesy of © 2009 Google

Figure C-14, Courtesy of © 2009 ZOHO Corp

Figure C-15, Courtesy of © 2009 Cisco WebEx LLC and/or its affiliated entities. All Rights Reserved

Figure C-16, Courtesy of Concord-Carlisle Regional High School

Unit D

Figure D-1, Courtesy of A. H. Bounar

Figure D-3, Facebook, © 2009

Figure D-4, Facebook, © 2009

Figures D-5, D-5a Courtesy of © 2006-2009 Pipl

Figure D-6, Courtesy of © 2003-2009 MySpace.com. All Rights Reserved

Figures D-7, D-8 Courtesy of LinkedIn Corporation © 2009

Figure D-9, Courtesy of © 2009 International Association of Business Communicators

Figure D-10, Courtesy of © 1995 - 2010 IAEE, All Rights Reserved

Figure D-11, Courtesy of © 2009 Sermo, Inc. All Rights Reserved

Figure D-12, Courtesy of © Technorati, Inc.

Figure D-13, Courtesy of Creative Commons (www.creativecommons.org)

Figure D-14a Courtesy of MT Cozzola

Figure D-15, Courtesy of Ilana Manolson and Christine Southworth

Figure D-16, Courtesy of © 2009 Created by WPS

Acknowledgements

Author Acknowledgements

We'd like to thank Brandi Shailer, Associate Acquisitions Editor, and Marjorie Hunt, Executive Editor, for taking our idea for a Web 2.0 book and running with it. We'd also like to thank Christina Kling Garrett, Senior Product Manager, for her skill at guiding the book through its many stages, and Product Manager Louise Capulli and Content Project Manager Lisa Weidenfeld for getting the book through production and into its final format. Many thanks to John Freitas and Marianne Snow, who check the manuscript for technical errors, and to our copy editor, Camille Kiolbasa, and our proofreader, Chris Clark, for catching the things we missed. We'd also like to thank Kat Ryan for securing all the permissions for this title. Thanks to our reviewers Barry Dahl, Lake Superior College, Pat Rahmlow, Montgomery County Community College, and Eileen Kelly Gorman, Elwood Public Schools. Kim Klasner, Editorial Assistant, organized the reviewers and oversaw the instructor resources. Thanks Kim!

Jane Hosie-Bounar   I had a lot of fun researching this book, and hope that you have as much fun reading it. The Web is an exciting place, full of information, yes, but also boundless creativity. A special thanks to Barbara Waxer, friend, editor, and co-author, for her humor, energy, and keen intelligence. Thanks also to my family for supporting me when I stayed up too late or got up too early, and especially to M.H.B., who let me stalk—I mean, research—her on Facebook with very few complaints.

Barbara Waxer   Deep thanks to the multi-talented Jane Hosie-Bounar for inviting me to write the copyright unit for this wonderful book, and to my partner, Lindy, for always putting up with it all.

Read This Before You Begin

Frequently Asked Questions

Where are the Data Files?

This book has no Data Files. However, for Unit B, students are required to sign up for free accounts with jamendo.com and flickr.com. They should also have a digital photograph that they can upload. Make sure that students have permission to use the photograph, or that it complies with the image's Creative Commons license and terms of use.

Many of the Web sites visited in this book display ads that students can click on. We do not advise that they do this, especially if it is against your school's online policy.

Since the Web is a dynamic place, it's possible that some of the sites listed in this book are no longer available. If this is the case, use a search engine to find a site with a similar functionality.

Do I need to be connected to the Internet to complete the steps and exercises in this book?

Yes, the exercises in this book assume that your computer is connected to the Internet. If you are not connected to the Internet, see your instructor for information on how to complete the exercises.

UNIT A
Web 2.0

Research 2.0

Files You Will Need:
No files needed

Originally designed to make it easy to spread information over the Internet, the World Wide Web has grown in ways no one could have foreseen when it first hit the virtual world over 20 years ago. Its latest version is Web 2.0, a brave new World Wide Web, where users can create and shape content. The early Web was mostly static, and then later included limited interactive features such as forms, email links, and shopping carts. However, Web 2.0 is all about dynamic Web pages, collaboration, and social networking. You can use it to streamline your research, to share your work, and to connect with others interested in the same subjects. You can also use it as a tool for gathering, organizing, and documenting information. With Web 2.0, turning your initial research into a polished paper or presentation is easier than ever. You are a freshman at Mirabeau College in Colorado, where you are excited to be starting your first semester in a new school. Although you used the Web in high school, you know that your college professors will expect much more from you now, and you are determined to make the most of all of the Web resources available to you. You have found that one of the core course offerings has a specific focus that you know will be valuable to you: Building Success with Web 2.0 Tools, taught by Professor Nadia Ahmed.

OBJECTIVES

Understand Web 2.0
Understand research tools
Find the best sources
Find primary sources
Judge a source's validity
Bookmark and highlight
Take notes and get organized
Cite sources and create a bibliography

UNIT A
Web 2.0

Understanding Web 2.0

What is Web 2.0 and how does it differ from the Web you may be accustomed to? Basically, the latest version of the Web turns the read-only Web into a read/write Web. It is less about static viewing and more about participation. In addition, Web 2.0 offers more tools than ever before for research and collaboration. With the right approach, you can use it to guarantee your success in school and beyond. 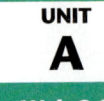 Your first assignment from Professor Ahmed is to research the ways Web 2.0 technologies can help you find, synthesize, and share information.

DETAILS

These are some of the Web 2.0 questions you want to answer:

- **What is Web 2.0?**

    You already know that the **World Wide Web** (commonly referred to as the Web) is a collection of Web sites, which, in turn, are made up of multiple Web pages connected via links that a user clicks to navigate. These Web pages reside on the **Internet**, a network of computers around the world. In the past, you could use the Web to get information, but unless you became a Web developer, that was where your participation stopped. **Web 2.0 technologies** give you, the user, the ability to collaborate with others, interact in **virtual** or online communities, and generate Web content yourself. Your participation in this new technology requires very little technical knowledge. If you have a device with an Internet connection, you can be a full member of this exciting and constantly changing new world. See Figure A-1 for some of the ways you can connect with Web 2.0 tools.

    > **QUICK TIP**
    > Do not click any online ads as you progress through the lessons in this book. They often have nothing to do with the Web 2.0 tool you are using, and might conflict with your school's online policies.

- **How have the research tools changed?**

    Web research tools have become more and more specialized. In the past, you often had to sift through hundreds—or even thousands—of Google search results to find exactly what you were looking for. Typing a search term like "Middle East" would take you to news, blog, mapping, and even restaurant and recipe sites. With Web 2.0, you can streamline your searches using the subject guides and special research engines discussed in this unit so that only valid research sources appear in your search results.

- **What collaboration tools are available?**

    You can always collaborate on projects by sending documents via email, sharing them via a flash drive, or posting them on an FTP site for your fellow students to download. However, with Web 2.0 technologies, you can store versions of your documents and presentations online so that your classmates can access and edit them in real time—as if you were all in a virtual conference room. See Figure A-2. Other Web 2.0 tools let you share notes, create your own research databases, and schedule meetings from any device with an Internet connection.

    > **QUICK TIP**
    > You should always keep in mind that if you are using collaboration tools on the Web, your information is public unless you have specified that it should be private or limited to a select group of users (for example, classmates).

- **What tools can help you organize your ideas?**

    Web 2.0 includes **mind-mapping software** (also sometimes called **note-taking software**) that lets you record information in the format that's best for you. If you are a visual learner, you might choose a tool that presents ideas in a graphic format using shapes and arrows. If you work better by organizing ideas under text headings, or in order of importance, there is a Web 2.0 tool for you as well. And, as you turn your notes into papers and presentations, you can use the Web 2.0 mapping features to help you organize complex ideas in a visual format so that you can easily see connections between ideas and data.

- **How can you use the Web to find media for your projects?**

    Because Web 2.0 lets you interact and share information with users from around the world, there is more media than ever available for papers, projects, and presentations. Anyone can post photos, videos, and audio files for others to see—but not necessarily use. Web sites like Flickr and Creative Commons are excellent starting points for finding media you can use in your projects. In addition, tools like Easybib, Ottobib, and Zotero help you keep track of your sources so that you can properly cite all references and media used in your research.

    > **QUICK TIP**
    > When you use media from the Internet in your projects, you should be aware that their use could involve complex permissions issues. Unit B, "Finding Media for Projects," covers copyright law and fair use issues in detail.

Research 2.0

FIGURE A-1: Connecting with Web 2.0 tools

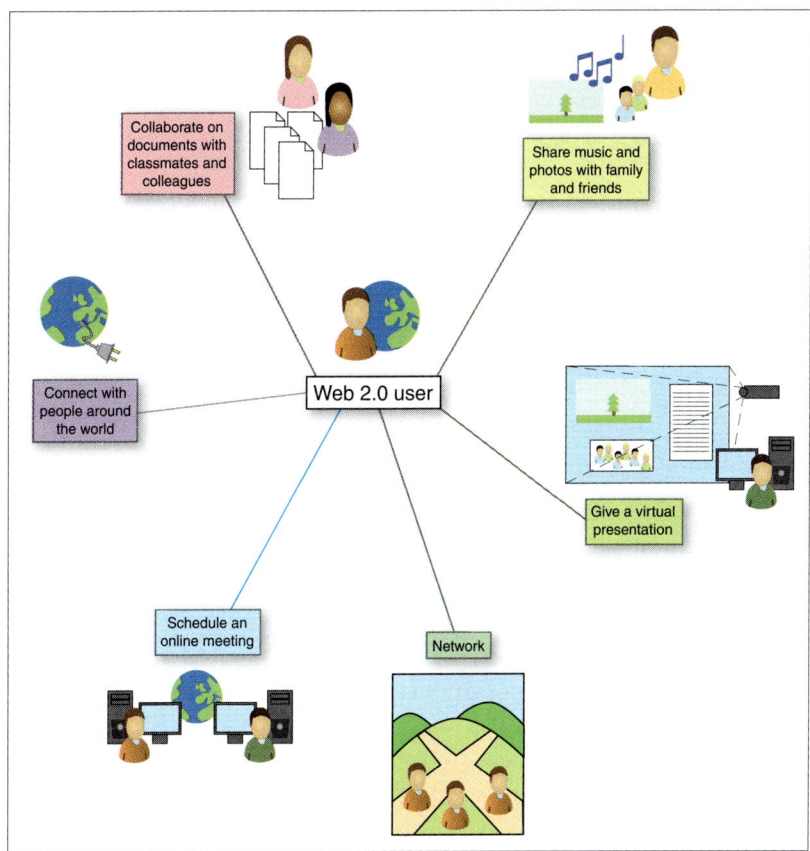

FIGURE A-2: Web 2.0 as a virtual conference room

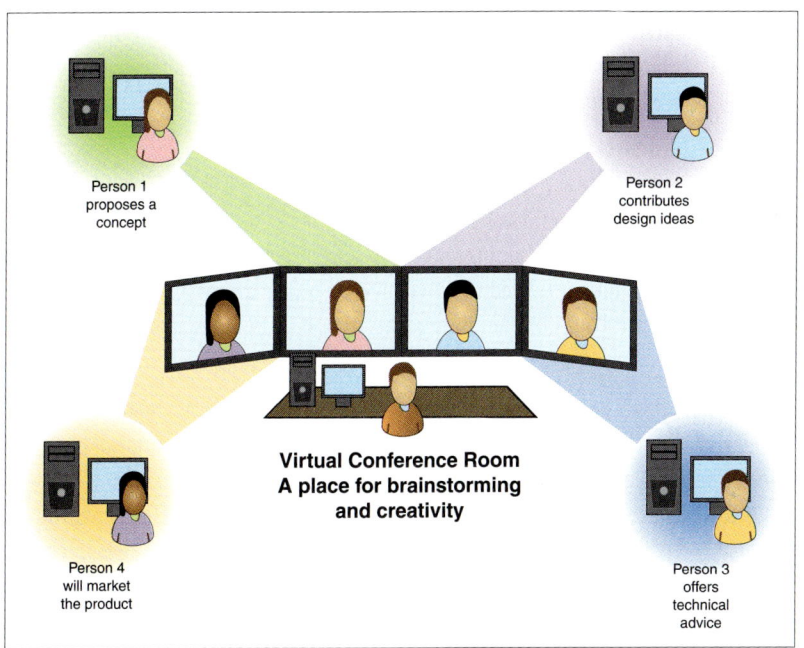

A word about privacy

The free exchange of information on the Web is a great thing, but it has its risks. Keep in mind that whatever you post on the Web is out there for the world to see unless you set some restrictions. You should also keep in mind that if you browse the Web or open email without having a firewall and virus protection installed on your computer, you are exposing all of the information on your computer to possible attacks, and yourself to possible identity theft. In addition, every new browser has a **phishing filter**, which lets you know when a Web site is suspect and might be attempting to steal your information while posing as your bank, credit card company, or "friend."

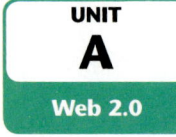

Understanding Research Tools

Not long ago, the best way to do research on almost any topic was to go to the library, thumb through a card catalog, find the subject you were interested in, find the titles of a few books, get their Dewey Decimal numbers, and then browse the library shelves to find them. Today, much of that grunt work can be done in an instant by typing a keyword or search term into a search engine and pressing [Enter] (Win) or [return] (Mac). Search engines like Google and Yahoo! are old standbys, but the Web also has more specialized and focused research tools, including subscription and nonsubscription databases and subject guides. See Table A-1 for a listing of many different kinds of research tools available to you. Professor Ahmed has asked the class to investigate and report on the different research tools available on the Web.

DETAILS

Common Web research tools include the following:

- **Search Engines**

    A **search engine** is a Web site that finds documents or media related to search terms or **keywords** that you provide. Common search engines include Google, Bing, AltaVista, Yahoo!, and Ask.com. There is also a category of search engine called a **meta-search engine**, which uses multiple search engines in a single search, and therefore returns more results. Meta-search engines include sites like Dogpile, Mamma, and Clusty. Most search engines will explain how they work on their Help pages, so you should be sure to read those before getting into any serious research project. For example, Clusty is a meta-search engine that prioritizes and groups search results into related "clusters" for easier navigation. Google worked with academic publishers to create a **specialized meta-search engine** named Google Scholar that finds the most up-to-date articles on almost any scholarly subject. Articles have been peer-reviewed by subject matter experts, so a search conducted with Google Scholar returns a shorter list of highly relevant results—with no sponsored links or advertisements. See Figure A-3.

- **Subject Guides**

    For more in-depth research you will have better success using a specialized search engine called a **subject guide**. Many school libraries create their own subject guides or subscribe to them on the Web. The advantage of a subject guide is that the information it contains is already categorized for you. For example, Figure A-4 shows a subject guide provided by the University of Delaware library. At the start of any research project, it is a good idea to ask your librarian if there are any subject guides available that are related to your topic.

- **Research Databases**

    A research **database** is a collection of data or links to data in many formats, including white papers and magazine, journal, and newspaper articles. You can feel relatively confident that the information you retrieve from a reputable database is accurate and has been reviewed by experts. You can search a research database to find specialized information because it is organized in a way that makes searching quick and intuitive. A **subscription database** is regularly updated by its owner and requires a fee to access. Often your school or public library will subscribe to multiple databases so that you can access that information for free. Ask your librarian what kinds of databases are available to you as a student at your school. If you are not in school, your public library can provide similar resources.

- **Online Catalogs**

    Online catalogs combine the resources of multiple libraries. WorldCat is one of the most well-known catalogs. **WorldCat** lists the resources of over 10,000 libraries worldwide. If you can't find a book you need, and your library is a member of WorldCat, you can order the book or other resource through your library's **interlibrary loan program** and it will arrive at your school within days. There is also a free version of the catalog online at www.worldcat.org. You can use it to find books in libraries near you, and to generate references for your bibliographies.

> **QUICK TIP**
>
> There are many **nonsubscription databases** on the Web. Some contain valuable information, but others don't necessarily contain peer-reviewed scholarly research. In the next lesson, you will learn how to judge the validity of information that you find on the Web.

Research 2.0

FIGURE A-3: Google search results versus Google Scholar search results

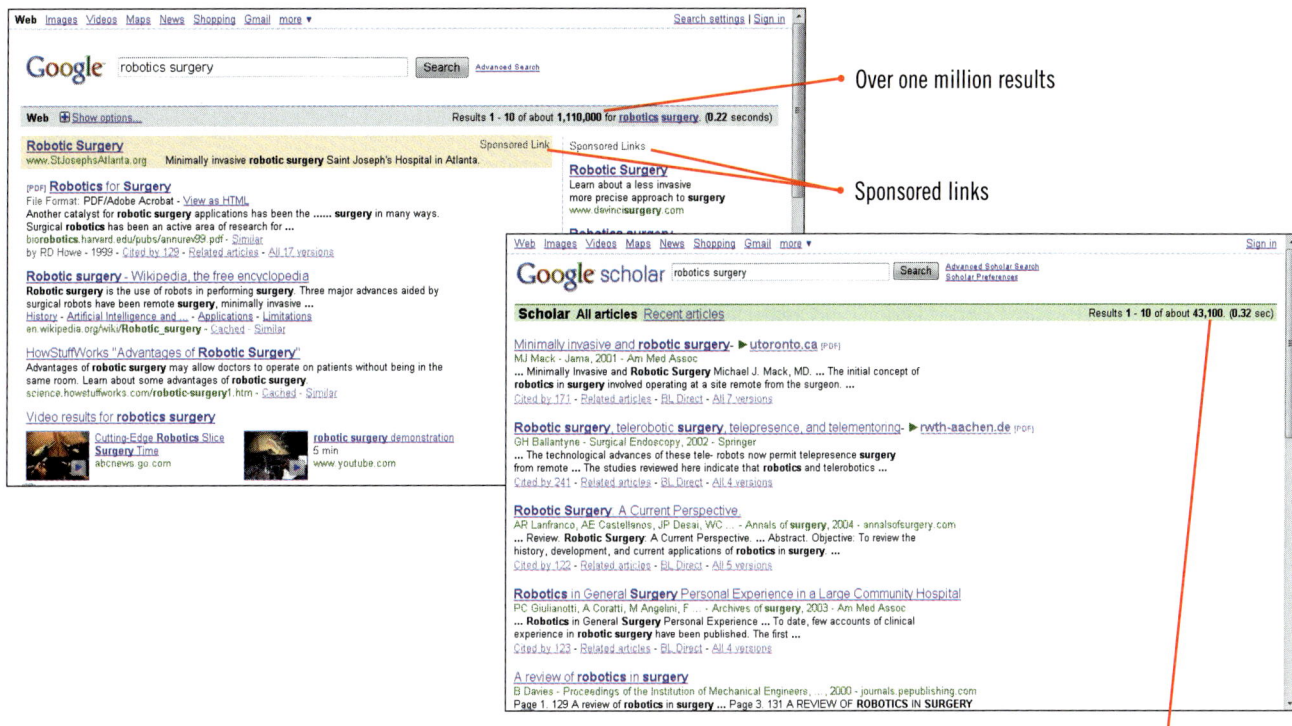

FIGURE A-4: University of Delaware subject guide

TABLE A-1: Popular research tools on the Web

Search Engines	Subject Guides	Research Databases	Online Catalogs
Search engines search the Web for media and information related to search terms or keywords that you provide.	Subject guides are generally created by libraries or public organizations. They are organized by category so that you can quickly click through a series of links to find your sources.	Research databases are organized by topic, and include links to subscribing libraries' journals, magazines, white papers, and articles.	Online catalogs are databases that record the contents of collections connected through an affiliation like a subscription. They do not contain the resources themselves, but provide references and cross-references to find what you're searching for.
Examples	**Examples**	**Examples**	**Examples**
Google, Yahoo!, Bing, Ask.com, AllTheWeb, and HotBot.	University library sites or academicinfo.net.	EBSCOhost and ERIC (for educational resources).	The Library of Congress Online Catalog and WorldCat.

Research 2.0

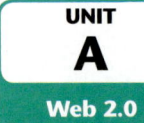

Finding the Best Sources

How do you narrow your search results to find the best sources? In general, the closer your source is to the topic or event itself, the more reliable it will be. You can look at the layers of information on the Web in terms of the game of telephone. We all know what happens to information that is funneled through many people: A simple sentence like "My hat is red" becomes "My cat is dead" by the time it has passed through all of the intermediate sources. The best way to get the real story in that game, of course, is to go to the primary source—or the person who spoke the sentence in the first place. Your professor has assigned a research paper about the Great Depression. Although the event took place well over half a century ago, she wants you to use the Web to find the main sources for your paper. First, however, you need to discover what kinds of sources will provide you with the best research and result in the strongest paper.

DETAILS

Sources on the Web can be classified into three categories, as shown in Figure A-5:

- **Primary Sources**

    Primary sources are documents, recordings, videos, or photographs created at the time of a particular event that you are writing about. For example, if you are researching a paper on the Great Depression in the 1930s, the photograph in Figure A-6, entitled "Destitute pea pickers in California," obtained from the Library of Congress Web site, is a primary source for your paper or presentation because it is a photograph actually taken during the Great Depression. For any research you are doing on American history and government, from Colonial times to the present, the Library of Congress Web site, at www.loc.gov, is an excellent resource for primary sources.

> **QUICK TIP**
> A primary source might also be the data from an experiment, compiled by the researcher, reviewed by peers, and then published on the Web.

- **Secondary Sources**

    Secondary sources discuss and analyze the information found in primary sources. For example, an article you might find on a Web site about the Great Depression that uses primary sources and then synthsizes them into an argument for or against government intervention in the economy would be a secondary source.

> **QUICK TIP**
> A secondary source might be another scientist's interpretation of data compiled by the original researcher.

- **Tertiary Sources**

    Tertiary sources are at least two steps removed from the primary source. An **encyclopedia**, which is the compilation of information from multiple primary and secondary sources, would be considered a tertiary source. Although a tertiary source like an encyclopedia might very well be a good place to start your research, it won't give you the depth and immediacy you need to create a strong research paper or presentation. If you start with a tertiary source, go directly to the primary or secondary sources it uses so that you can get the most reliable information. An excellent tertiary source that your school might subscribe to is World Book Online or World Book Kids, which not only lets you do research, but lets you put the information you find in a virtual "backpack."

FIGURE A-5: Sources on the Web

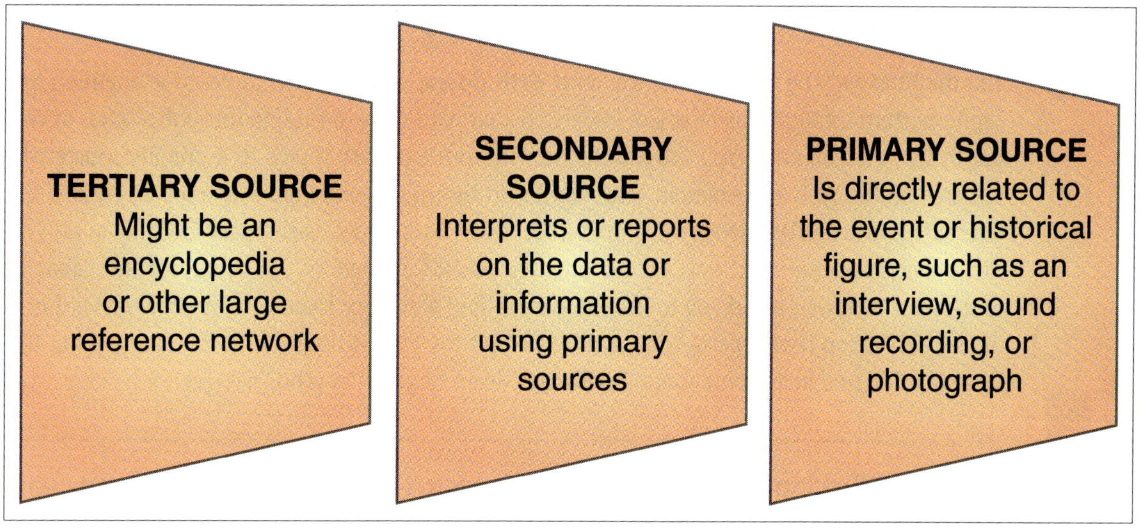

TERTIARY SOURCE
Might be an encyclopedia or other large reference network

SECONDARY SOURCE
Interprets or reports on the data or information using primary sources

PRIMARY SOURCE
Is directly related to the event or historical figure, such as an interview, sound recording, or photograph

FIGURE A-6: An example of a primary source

When books are best

You can find a great deal of information on the Web, but many people believe there is nothing like the satisfaction of holding a book, magazine, or newspaper in your hands and reading and studying its contents. A book on a particular subject covers that subject in depth, and to an extent you won't find on a Web page or even a series of Web pages. Furthermore, many books and journals have gone through a rigorous peer review process before being published, whereas information on the Web can be posted on the fly, without any review process at all. (Keep in mind, though, that with the advent of "vanity" or self-publishing sites, there are books that have not been peer-reviewed—or even copyedited or proofread. You should check a book's publisher before deciding to use it in a research project.) If you are looking for a book, keep in mind that the Web is an excellent place to start your search. Many research databases will point you directly to hard copy sources like books, providing you with title, author, publisher, Dewey Decimal number, or even an **ISBN (International Standard Book Number)**, which is a unique number assigned to a publication that ensures that you can find the edition you are looking for. In addition, you can download **e-books**, which are electronic versions of traditional printed books, and read them on your PC or on a handheld electronic reading device like **Kindle**.

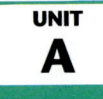

UNIT A
Web 2.0

Finding Primary Sources

You might already be familiar with the term **drill down**, which is used to describe anything from moving top to bottom through a hierarchy of folders on your hard drive to clicking through a series of Web pages to get to the one you need. You can also drill down from a tertiary source to a primary source when you do research on the Web. For example, you might start by typing a keyword into a search engine, then clicking a tertiary source like Wikipedia, moving to a secondary source, and then finally locating an original photo or document from the event you are researching. As part of your study of the Great Depression, Professor Ahmed has asked you to use the Web to find a primary source about a major event or personality in the 1930s. You have recently seen a movie about the FBI's struggles with the gangsters of the time and you are interested in learning about the life and death of gangster John Dillinger.

STEPS

Take the following steps to find a primary source for a subject that interests you:

1. **Type a keyword or keywords into a search engine, database, or subject guide**

   For example, typing John Dillinger into the Google search engine displays thousands of results. Note that some search results include a misspelling of his last name.

   > **QUICK TIP**
   > To open a link in a new browser tab, press and hold [Ctrl] (Win) or [command] (Mac), then click a link. This way, you can easily open links of interest as you keep the search results open.

2. **Open a tertiary source link that interests you in a new tab**

   The example in Figure A-7 shows the Wikipedia Web page for John Dillinger. Wikipedia is a good example of what Web 2.0 technology has added to the process of gathering and sharing information. The word **Wikipedia** is a combination of the words "wiki" and "encyclopedia." A **wiki** is a collaborative Web site, where users can post information and edit each other's work. An **encyclopedia** is a comprehensive collection of articles on different topics ranging from anthropology to history to zoology. However, you should be aware that Wikipedia differs from a traditional encyclopedia in a number of ways. It is not issued by a central publisher, nor does it go through a traditional review process. Rather, it is written, edited, and constantly updated by the Web community. This means that it can contain a wealth of information, but it also means that some of the information might be inaccurate, incomplete, or even intentionally misleading.

3. **Determine if the Web page lists any secondary or primary sources**

   Most Wikipedia entries have Works cited, Further reading, and External links sections at the bottom of the page. Other Web sites will also include external links that you can follow.

   > **QUICK TIP**
   > Many instructors will not accept Wikipedia as a source in your bibliography or works cited because the article is not a primary or secondary source. This policy ensures that your research is accurate.

4. **Make a note of the works cited or further reading suggestions so that you can continue your research in more depth, then open a secondary link in a new tab**

   At the bottom of the Dillinger entry, there is a link to a book called *On the Lam: Narratives of Flight in J. Edgar Hoover's America*. Clicking the link takes you to the publisher's Web site, where you can purchase the book or use the title, author, and ISBN information to find the book in your school or public library.

5. **Open additional links as desired**

   Some links from Wikipedia might take you to Web pages of questionable value. Others might take you to education or government Web sites or to the Web sites of book publishers. You can use the information in the next lesson to help you determine whether or not the sources you have uncovered are valid.

6. **Open any external links leading to .gov or .edu sites in a new tab**

   These sites often include primary sources. In the Dillinger example, clicking the link shown in Figure A-7 takes you to the FBI site titled Famous Cases: John Dillinger.

   > **TROUBLE**
   > If your first attempt at finding a primary source doesn't yield results, don't give up. Some research requires quite a bit of digging before you succeed.

7. **Explore the links for primary sources**

   Clicking the "FBI case records" link in the For more information section at the bottom of the FBI Web page and then drilling down by clicking additional links takes you to the primary source shown in Figure A-8.

Research 2.0

FIGURE A-7: Wikipedia page for John Dillinger

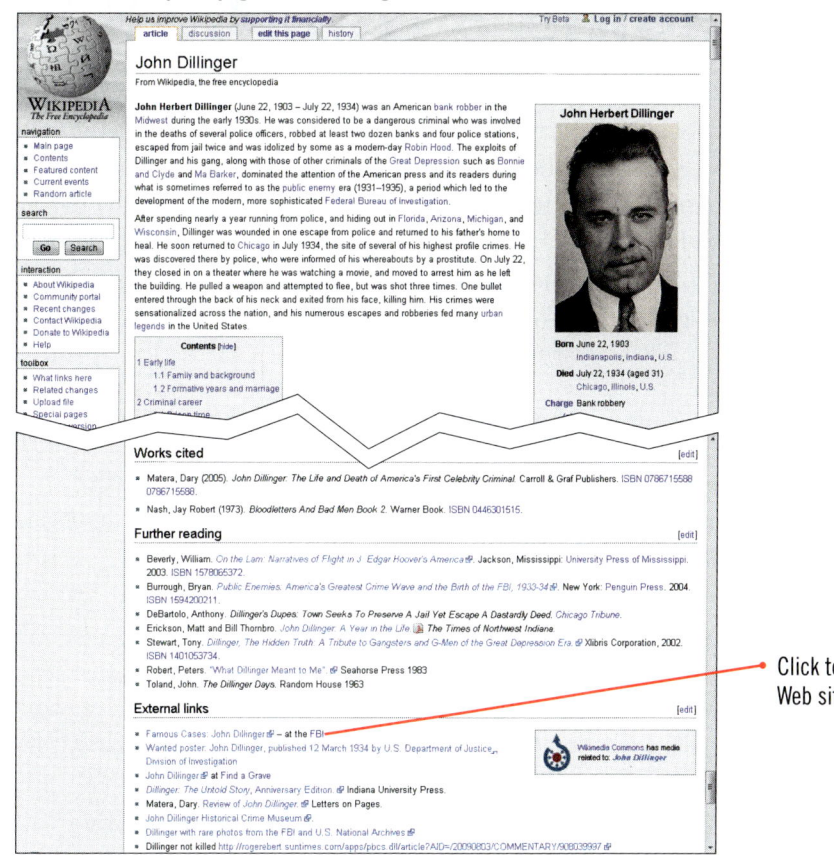

FIGURE A-8: Primary source for John Dillinger research

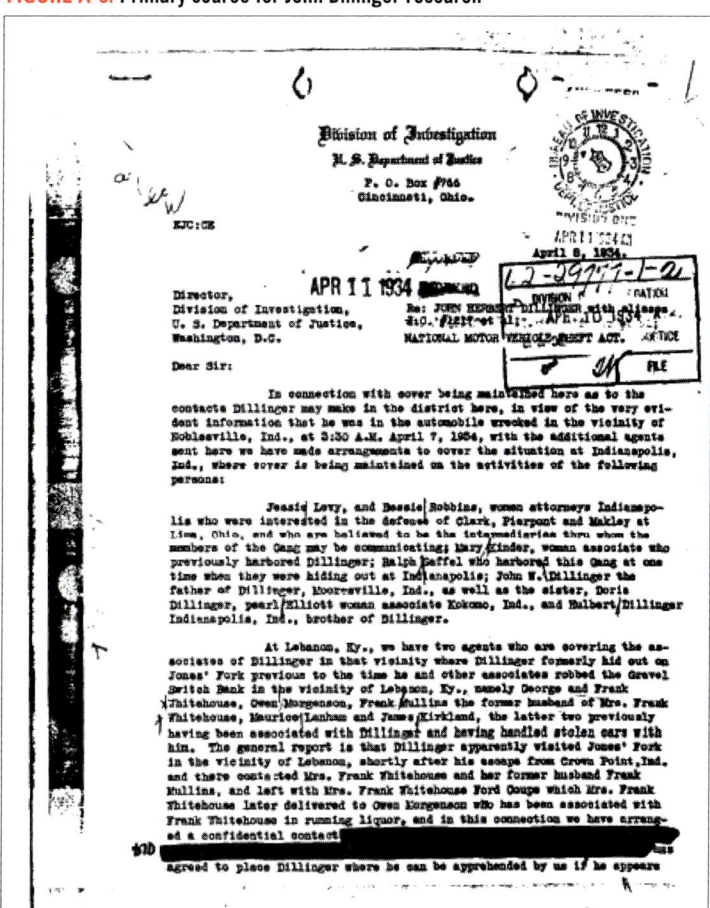

UNIT A
Web 2.0

Judging a Source's Validity

When you use the Web for research, you have thousands of references at your fingertips. It might seem that the amount of information you can find on any topic is limitless. However, because Web 2.0 lets anyone post information, how can you be sure that every article or Web site you find in your research has been **vetted**, or checked for accuracy by a subject matter expert? The truth is, you can't be sure, but there are ways to judge the validity of a source so that you can use it in your research with confidence. 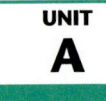 Professor Ahmed has asked you to develop a list of ways to determine whether a source is valid. You decide that you will create a list of questions to help you choose sources.

DETAILS

When determining the validity of a source, ask yourself the following questions:

- **Is the reference a primary, secondary, or tertiary source?**
  As you learned in the previous lesson, the distance of a source from the original event or historical person can be an indication of its value to your project.

> **QUICK TIP**
> Sources returned by Google Scholar are always peer-reviewed.

- **Is the Web site for the source reputable?**
  You should always be a little skeptical of any information you find on the Web, but as a general rule, you can trust the veracity and accuracy of university and government Web sites, and sites that have a system of peer review or a long-standing reputation in the industry. For example, if you need information on how to treat a spider bite, a reliable medical Web site such as WebMD.com would be a better resource than a Web site that has a person's name in the URL whose background is unknown.

- **Does the Web site for the source have an ulterior motive?**
  Be wary of any site with a .com in its domain name. It may be a commercial Web site trying to sell you a product rather than providing objective information. For example, if you are writing a report on the correlation between loud music and hearing loss, stay away from any .com site that claims "research has shown that our earbuds not only improve your listening experience but reverse hearing loss caused by years of inferior headphones." In this case, you should find the research, identify the researchers and their affiliations, and make your own judgment. Furthermore, if you do determine that the claim has some validity, you should use the research itself in your paper, and not the claim by the company.

> **QUICK TIP**
> To find information that is posted only on education Web sites, you can go to SearchEdu.com, a specialized search engine that returns only Web pages posted on school and university Web sites.

- **What is the domain of the Web site?**
  A Web site's address uses words and abbreviations to make it easy to remember. For example, www.nps.gov is the address or **domain name** of the National Park Service (NPS). The last letters in a domain name, to the right of the period, are called the **top-level domain (TLD)**. In this case, the .gov TLD indicates that the Web site is a government site. Table A-2 lists top-level domains and their meanings. Be aware that open TLDs can be used by anyone.

- **Do other sources confirm the information?**
  Never rely on a single resource for your "facts." Starting at one site and then searching other sites to determine if there is consensus on a claim will strengthen your research and may uncover errors that you wouldn't have been aware of otherwise. For example, a quick Google search on the question "How many moons does Jupiter have?" yields different results, ranging from 16 moons to 63 moons. See Figure A-9. Posing the same question at the NASA Web site gives a more reliable answer, as shown in Figure A-10.

- **Is the author of the source an expert on the subject?**
  Because anyone can post information on the Web, you need to verify the identity and credentials of the author of any source you plan to use. Does the author hold an advanced degree in the field he or she is writing about? Is the author cited by other experts in the field? If the Web site where you find the source lists author credentials, read them. Is the author affiliated with an institution such as a university or a teaching hospital?

- **Is it possible to contact the author or organization?**
  Any information you find should lead you to the author or organization responsible for posting it. Use any contact information to get additional facts, or to further evaluate the source of the information.

Research 2.0

FIGURE A-9: A search finds different answers to the same question

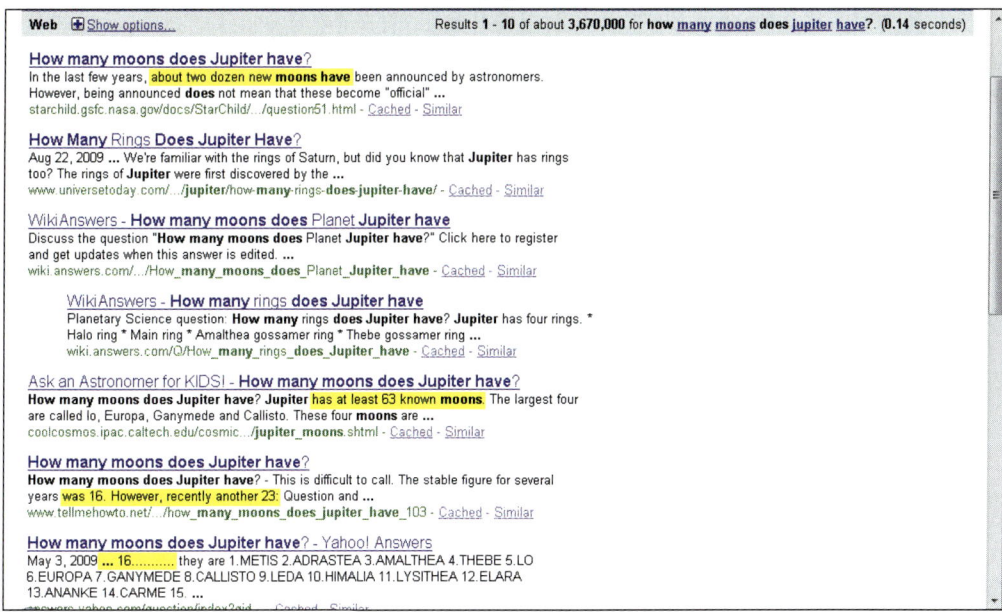

FIGURE A-10: NASA site is a reliable source for the Jupiter moons question

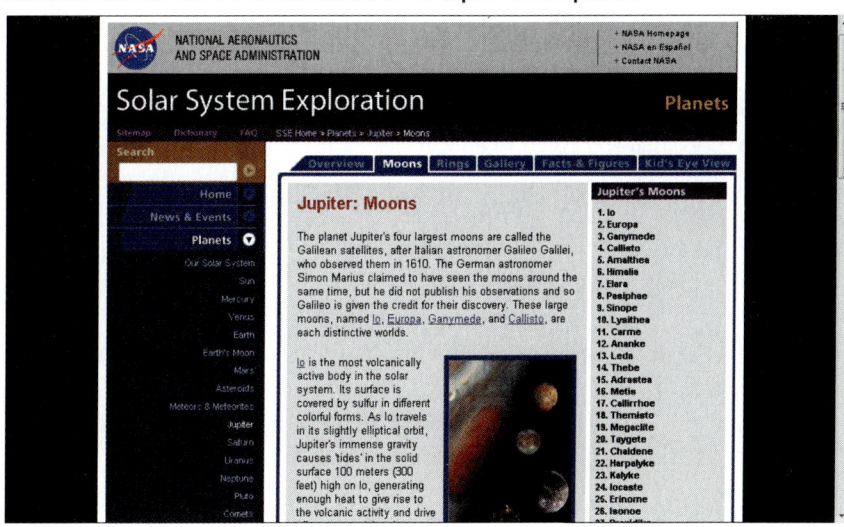

TABLE A-2: Top-level domains and their meanings

top-level domain (TLD)	kind
biz	business
com	commercial
edu	educational
gov	U.S. government
info	TLD has no specific meaning; anyone can use it
mil	U.S. military
museum	museums
net	TLD has no specific meaning; anyone can use it
org	TLD has no specific meaning; anyone can use it
pro	professional (for licensed or certified professionals like lawyers, engineers, doctors)
au, uk, ca, cn, fr	country domains: Australia, United Kingdom, Canada, China, France

Research 2.0

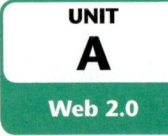

Bookmarking and Highlighting

Storing a Web address as a **bookmark** in Firefox or Safari or as a **favorite** in Internet Explorer makes it easy to return to a Web site that you find useful. However, a browser only stores a bookmark locally on your computer, which makes it difficult to access that same information from a library or classroom computer, or from the laptop of someone in your study group. If you use Web 2.0 bookmarks, you can return to your favorite Web sites from any computer. You can also use Web 2.0 **highlighting tools** to go one step further and highlight important information on a Web page just as you would highlight information in a book or article. See Table A-3 for a list of bookmarking sites. Professor Ahmed posts information for her course on three different Web sites. One stores a class syllabus, one is a class blog, and the other is a wiki where her students can share notes and comment about each day's lecture. She suggests that you find out how bookmarking and highlighting tools will help you keep track of multiple sites not only for her class, but for all of your courses.

DETAILS

You can work with bookmarking and highlighting tools in the following ways:

- **Using personal bookmarks**

    Web 2.0 bookmarks use a method called **tagging** to let you retrieve previously visited sites using words or phrases (**tags**) that you assign when you create the bookmark. Tags (also called **labels**) save you the trouble of going through your list of bookmarks each time you want to find a particular one. For example, if you take five classes, each associated with three or four Web sites that you have bookmarked for class research, and also use sites like Facebook and iTunes, your bookmark list can get quite long. If you assign a tag such as WebTools for your technology class and AmLit for your literature class, you can narrow down your list by typing in the appropriate tag to see only the sites associated with the tagged class. You can also create bookmarks for specific projects you are working on. For example, any research on the gangster John Dillinger turns up quite a few useful Web sites. You can bookmark these sites in software like Google Bookmarks using the label "Dillinger" so that they are always easily accessible. See Figure A-11 for a complete list of user bookmarks, and the same list after the bookmarks are searched on "dillinger."

> **QUICK TIP**
> Many online bookmarking tools let you import your local bookmarks from your browser. When you add or delete a bookmark online, the change is also made to your local bookmarks, and vice versa.

- **Highlighting bookmarked information**

    Many bookmarking sites also let you highlight the information you have found, just as you would highlight words or phrases in a book. The highlights you make on a page don't disappear when you leave the site, although other visitors to the site can't see them. Highlighting software saves the highlights with your account so that they are still there for you when you use a bookmark to return to the site to continue your research at another time. As shown in Figure A-12, using highlighting, you don't need to reread an entire article or resource to find the information that made you bookmark the site in the first place. The highlight you added to the site draws your eyes to the information you considered important.

> **QUICK TIP**
> Some highlighting and bookmarking tools even let you put "sticky notes" or comments directly on a Web page.

- **Sharing bookmarks**

    Social bookmarks are bookmarks that you share with friends, classmates, or with the entire Web community. Social bookmarking sites include Delicious.com, Stumbleupon.com, Diigo.com, Yahoo! Buzz, and Digg, among others. To learn how to share your bookmarks, consult the site's Help or About Web page.

> **QUICK TIP**
> Some social bookmarking sites let you post small bits of text or images from other Web sites so that you can share your interests with others. Sites such as Clipmarks.com let registered users click a "clip" and "follow" it to the original site.

FIGURE A-11: One user's Google bookmarks before and after "dillinger" search

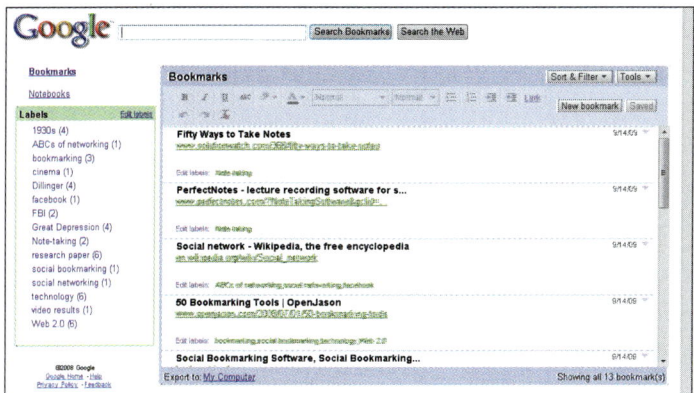

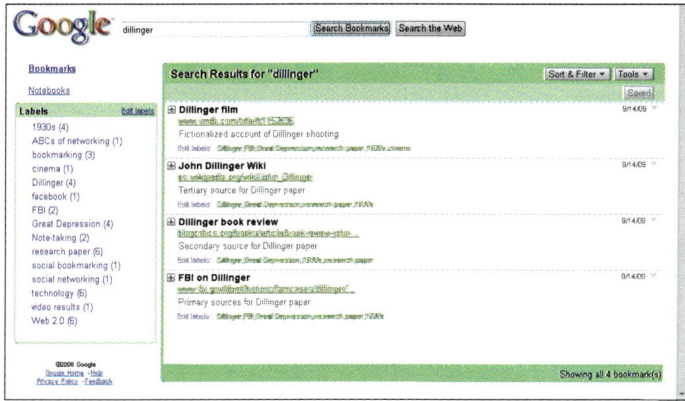

FIGURE A-12: Highlighted article from FBI site

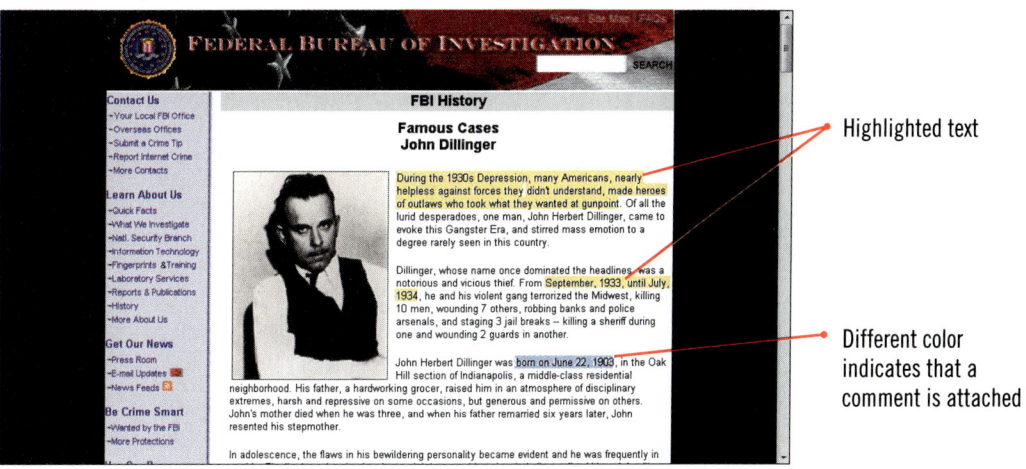

TABLE A-3: Bookmarking sites

site	benefits	sharing	highlighting	commenting
Clipmarks (Clipmarks.com)	tag and organize in folders, embed clips on other sites	Yes	No	Yes
amplify (amplify.com)	"clip" and share content, archive Web content	Yes	No	Yes
Diigo (Diigo.com)	import bookmarks, tag pages, search text and comments	Yes	Yes	Yes
Delicious (Delicious.com)	Import bookmarks, tag pages, share bookmarks with others	Yes	No	No

Research 2.0

Taking Notes and Getting Organized

Some of the most exciting Web 2.0 tools are designed with students in mind. For example, mind-mapping software lets you take notes and then reorganize the information to create study guides or outlines. You can record key points during a biology lecture in the morning, save your notes to the Web, and then access them later from a library desktop for a late-night study session. In order to fully comprehend the information in your notes, you can use the mapping features of the software to reorganize the information in a linear or graphic manner so that it makes the most sense to you. Gathering and processing information in this way reinforces the concepts you learn during a lecture or reading, and ensures success in your classes. Professor Ahmed wants you to explore the ways that mind-mapping software can help you record and organize your research.

DETAILS

These are the questions you should ask yourself once you have finished your research:

> **QUICK TIP**
> The functions of note-taking and mind-mapping software sometimes overlap, but, in general, note-taking software lets you jot down ideas that you can save to the Web for later access. Mind-mapping software has more organization features, and mixes graphics and text.

- ### What do I do with all of this information?
  You have finished the research on your topic and have gathered your sources together using bookmarks and highlighting tools. Your sources include lecture notes, Web pages, articles, photographs, and books in the form of primary, secondary, and tertiary sources. How do you organize all of this information and get down to the business of writing? You could page through the information, picking up bits and pieces here and there and laying them out as you write, but your progress would most likely be pretty slow. You need tools to help you put information in your own words, process that information, and then organize it in a way that makes sense to you.

- ### What tools can I use to take notes?
  After you have gathered your sources, you should take extensive notes on your subject using a Web 2.0 mind-mapping tool. A **mind-mapping tool** helps you record information in a format that works for you, revise the information to put it into your own words, and reorganize it in a linear or graphical way, depending on your learning style.

  Some sites like mindmeister.com let you use mind-mapping tools online, while others require you to download them in order to use them. Figure A-13 shows two examples of a mind map. It is up to you to determine which format works best. For example, if you learn better by making lists and reading key points and summaries, you might want a text-based tool. If you prefer to see your information laid out in a diagram that shows relationships, you should probably use a tool based on diagramming.

- ### What is the best way to assimilate the information?
  The notes you take during lectures and readings can be used for many things. You might be tested on the material you have taken notes on, or you might be required to produce a paper or presentation based on what you have learned. The best way to make sure you understand the information before you are tested on it or need to present it is to review your notes, and then reorganize them. The sooner you do this after a lecture or reading, the more likely you are to remember the information later. As you review your notes, figure out what kind of organization will help you highlight key points or trends, and then use mind mapping to put your notes into that form. If you spend enough time working with your research or notes in this way, your exam or paper will almost write itself.

FIGURE A-13: Two examples of mind maps created with NovaMind (www.novamind.com) and Visual Mind (www.visual-mind.com)

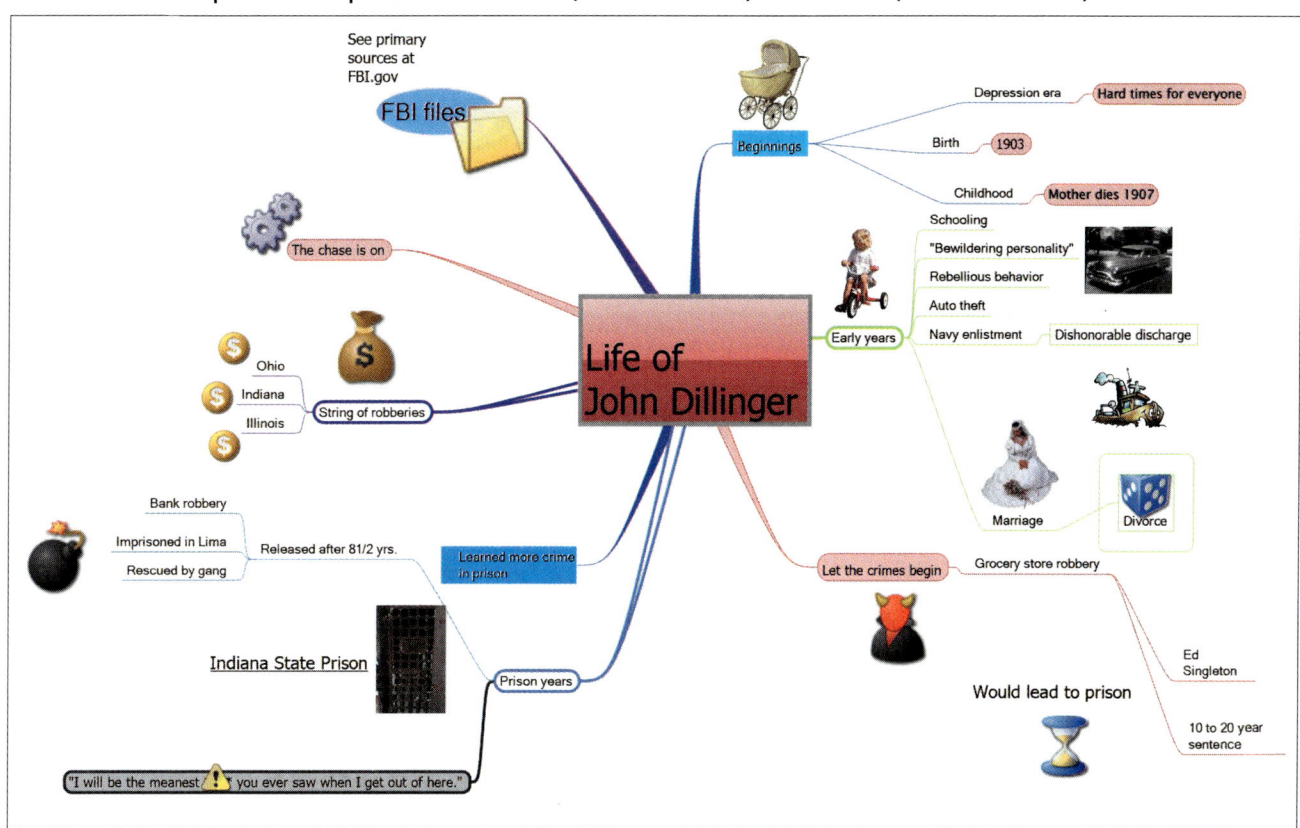

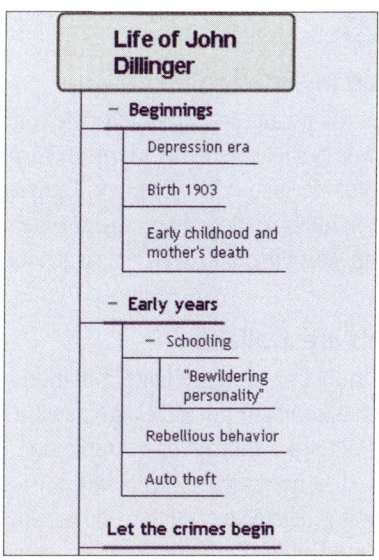

Dealing with writer's block

If you have made it this far in your education, you probably already know what writer's block is. It happens at the moment you sit down to write that paper you have done so much research on. You've been living with the topic for days or weeks and have exhausted all of your resources. You are as much of an expert on the topic as you will ever be. Today, however, you find you have absolutely nothing to say about it. What is the best way to handle this situation? Do you stare at a blank computer screen? Go for a walk? Update your social networking page? The best way to overcome writer's block is to take it by storm—that is, **brainstorm**: Write an outline on paper or online. Start with an introduction. Summarize your main point or argument in a **thesis**. Write a series of **topic sentences** for each paragraph that support your thesis. Put them in order. Reorder them. See what organization will most likely lead to the conclusion you're aiming for. *Then* take your walk and think about something else. When you return to your computer, you'll find that the hardest part of your job is already done.

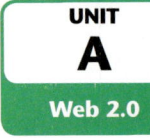

Citing Sources and Creating a Bibliography

With all of the free access to information on the Web, it is sometimes easy to forget that someone had to report on the information in the first place, and deserves credit. As you work on any research project, you should keep a list of your sources so that you don't forget to **cite**, or credit, them when you submit your work. In the past, you had to type out your sources and then organize them in a reference list called a **bibliography**. Using the Web, however, you can now get your bibliography (also called a **Works Cited list**) generated for you using a few simple steps. Before you sit down to write your research paper, you want to make sure you have the right tools to make creating a bibliography as easy as possible.

DETAILS

Web 2.0 provides a number of ways to keep track of and then generate a bibliography for your sources:

QUICK TIP
See Unit B, "Finding Media for Projects," for a comprehensive discussion on when to cite a source, and when permission is required.

- **How do you determine what information needs to be credited?**
  Sometimes it will be obvious to you when you need to credit a source. For example, if you are using a **direct quotation** from the source, that source should appear in your bibliography. There are also gray areas when it comes to citing sources. For example, if you **paraphrase** an idea presented in a source by taking the idea and putting it in your own words, it is still not your idea and should be credited. Other information, however, is considered general knowledge. For example, if you are writing a paper about the Herbert Hoover presidency and say that Herbert Hoover was president of the United States when the stock market crashed, that is something that would be considered **general knowledge**, or knowledge that is available to anyone, and it would not need to be cited. See Figure A-14.

- **What format should my citation take?**
  Your professor or school will usually specify which style your bibliography should use. Most Web 2.0 bibliography generators give you a choice of style. Many Word processors have built-in tools to do this as well. Common reference styles include MLA (Modern Language Association), APA (American Psychological Association), Chicago, or Turabian. Before you spend time searching the Web for a citation generator that's right for you, check with your librarian to see if your school subscribes to a comprehensive tool like EasyBib or NoodleBib.

- **What Web 2.0 tools are available?**
  Some generators, like OttoBib, are free, but have limitations—for example, they might only generate bibliographies using MLA format, or might not have automated features like ISBN entry. Others, like EasyBib, provide limited functionality unless you pay for a subscription. The bibliography entry generated by OttoBib in Figure A-15 was produced by typing a book ISBN into the tool and clicking a button. The bibliography entry shown in Figure A-16 was generated by copying and pasting a URL into a text box on bibme.org. You might find that a single tool can handle all of your sources, from magazine articles to books to Web sites, or you might find that a combination of tools works best for you.

A word about plagiarism

There are countless ethical reasons why plagiarism is wrong. In the first place, you are stealing someone's property. It might not be an iPod or a gold chain that you've taken, but you have taken something of great value: intellectual property. Furthermore, your professor assigns papers and projects so that you can learn. If you plagiarize by stealing someone else's work, or by buying a paper from a Web site, you've learned nothing. If these arguments haven't convinced you not to plagiarize, here's another one: The existence of search engines on the Web will ensure that you will get caught. All a professor has to do is copy a sentence or a paragraph from your paper into a search engine, and the source of "your" work is bound to appear in the search results. Some professors even subscribe to Web sites that let them run entire papers through their software in order to check for questionable authorship.

FIGURE A-14: When to cite a source

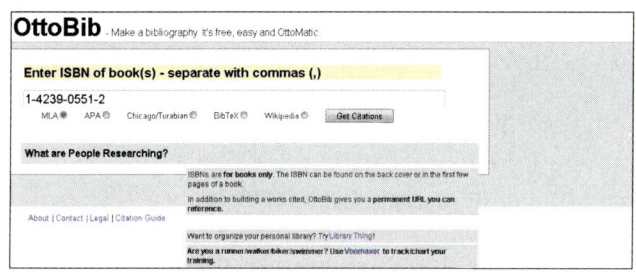

FIGURE A-15: Automatically generated book citation in MLA format

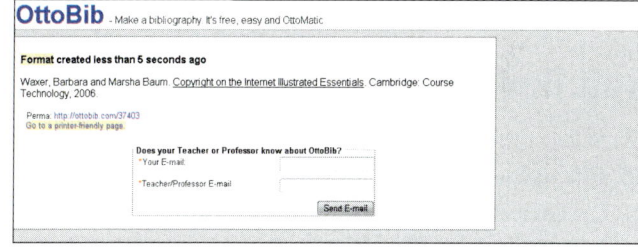

FIGURE A-16: Automatically generated citation for a Web site

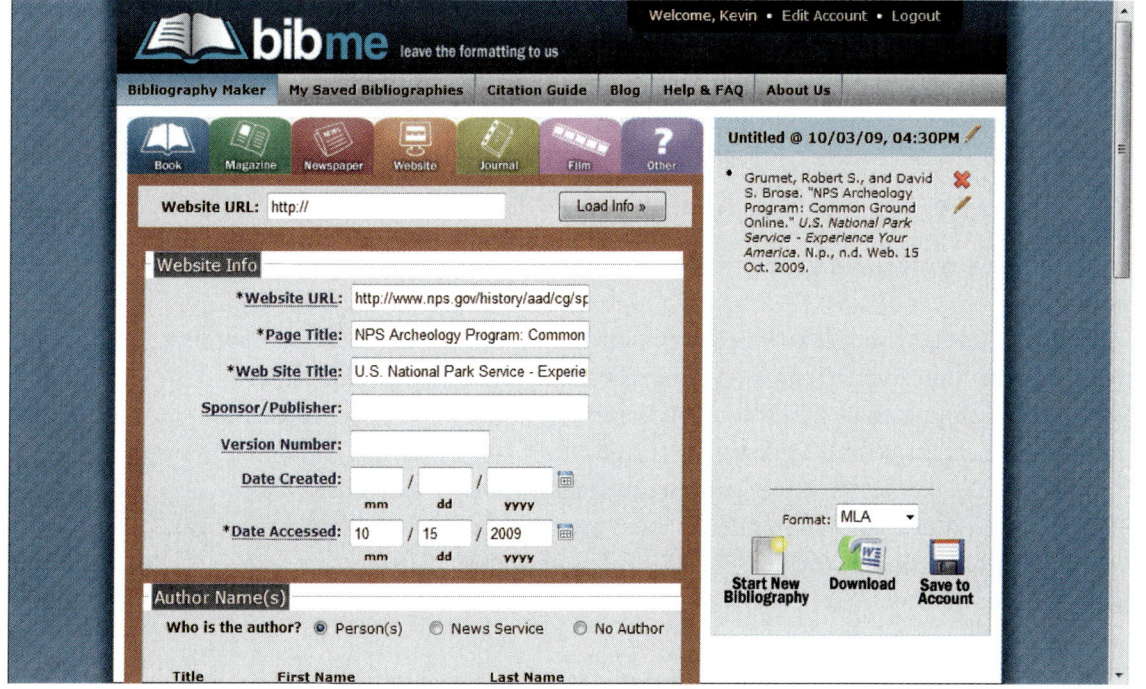

Research 2.0

Practice

Key Terms

bibliography	highlighting tools	phishing filter	tertiary source
bookmark	interlibrary loan program	plagiarism	thesis
brainstorm	Internet	primary source	topic sentences
cite	ISBN	research database	top-level domain (TLD)
direct quotation	keyword	search engine	vetted
domain name	Kindle	secondary source	virtual
drill down	labels	social bookmarks	Web 2.0 technology
e-book	meta-search engine	subject guide	wiki
encyclopedia	mind-mapping software	subscription database	Wikipedia
favorite	nonsubscription databases	tagging	works cited
general knowledge	note-taking software	tags	World Wide Web
hard copy	paraphrase		

Unit Review

1. What are the key new features of Web 2.0 technologies, and how do they differ from Web 1.0?
2. Discuss some things you should consider before sharing information on the Web.
3. Give three examples of research tools.
4. What is the difference between a search engine and a meta-search engine?
5. What are the benefits of a subject guide?
6. Discuss the difference between a primary source, a secondary source, and a tertiary source, and give examples of each.
7. Name three things you should consider when you try to determine whether or not a source is valid.
8. What is the difference between a personal bookmark and a social bookmark?
9. What is a mind map and what are its benefits?
10. Give three examples of information that requires you to cite a source.

Fill in the best answer

1. If you can't find a resource in your own library, you can order it through your school's _____ loan program.
2. To move from a tertiary source to a primary source, you can _____ down by clicking links.
3. A unique number that identifies a book and its edition is called a(n) _____.
4. The process of adding tags or labels to a bookmarking Web site in order to classify your bookmarks is called _____.
5. _____ _____ lets you use diagrams and text to summarize and organize information.
6. _____ is when you take someone else's idea and put it into your own words.
7. The three-letter extension at the end of a Web site's address is called a(n) _____.
8. When an article has been checked by experts, it has been _____.

9. The feature that lets people work together by sharing information and editing work online is called _____.

10. A collection of data or links to data and articles is called a(n) _____ _____.

Select the best answer from the list of choices.

1. Which is an example of a primary source?
    a. An article about the Emancipation Proclamation.
    b. A Wikipedia entry about the Emancipation Proclamation.
    c. The diary of an emancipated slave.
    d. A film about the signing of the Emancipation Proclamation.
2. What is NOT a benefit of a subscription database?
    a. It is regularly updated.
    b. It requires an access fee.
    c. It is peer-reviewed.
    d. It is organized into subcategories.
3. What is a personal bookmark?
    a. A reference to a Web site that you share with friends.
    b. A reference to a Web site that you share with the Web community.
    c. A highlight that marks important information on your blog.
    d. A marker for your own use that lets you return to a Web site from your browser.
4. What is a tag?
    a. A word or phrase that you use to categorize your bookmarks.
    b. A bibliography entry.
    c. Highlighting software.
    d. Another word for a domain name.
5. Which of the following is a tertiary source?
    a. Merriam Webster Dictionary.
    b. The World Book Encyclopedia.
    c. Wikipedia.
    d. All of the above.
6. Which top-level domain is not necessarily a good one to use for research?
    a. .com
    b. .gov
    c. .org
    d. None of the above.
7. What is a subject guide?
    a. A study guide created with mind-mapping software.
    b. A meta-search engine.
    c. A bookmarking tool.
    d. The hard copy version of an academic journal.
8. What does a phishing filter do?
    a. Narrows your search results so that they are more manageable.
    b. Filters your bookmarks by subject.
    c. Collects highlighted material in a single document.
    d. Protects you from data and identity theft.

Independent Challenge 1

You are helping your professor with his research on robotics engineering. He has asked you to find articles on the uses of robotics in space exploration. (*Note*: Please check with your instructor for assignment submission instructions. If you cannot post your solution files, your instructor might want you to save them and then email them.)

   a. Start your research by selecting one of the popular search engines, such as Google or Bing.
   b. Open a new file in a word processor, then save the file as **Robotics in Space**.
   c. Search on the keywords **robotics** and **space exploration**, then note the number of results.
   d. Create a three-column table, click three of the search results in your browser, then type their URLs in the first column of the table.

Independent Challenge 1 (continued)

    e. Interpret the top-level domain letters of each site, then type which kind they are in column 2. For example, if the domain is .com, type Commercial.

    f. In column 3, write whether the site would be a primary, secondary, or tertiary source for your research and explain why.

    g. Type **your name**, save and close Robotics in Space, then exit the word processor.

    h. Post the file online in the location specified by your instructor. (*Hint*: The location should be a private location, not a public Web site.)

Independent Challenge 2

You have a job in the community outreach department of a local art museum. The museum has recently been added to an international tour of Francisco de Goya paintings, and you are responsible for writing an educational guide about Goya for schoolchildren. You decide to use a subject guide on the Web to find information about Goya. (*Note*: Please check with your instructor for assignment submission instructions.)

    a. Go to www.google.com, then search on the terms **humanities** and **subject guides**.

    b. Click the link to one of the subject guides.

    c. Drill down in the subject guide until you get to the art category, and then drill further until you find information about Goya. (*Hint*: You may need to experiment with different sites.)

    d. Print the Web page, use the screen capture tool of your choice to capture the page, or save it as **Goya Research**. Post it online in the location specified by your instructor or email the file to your instructor.

    e. Find digital images of three of Goya's paintings. Print the Web pages or use the screen capture tool of your choice to capture the images, then post them online in the location specified by your instructor.

Independent Challenge 3

You and your best friend at school are looking for summer jobs. You both agree that you'd like to spend most of your time outside. You decide you'll use Web 2.0 tools to find jobs in the National Park Service. (*Note*: You can print or post this assignment. Please check with your instructor for assignment submission instructions.)

    a. Open a document in a word processor, save it as **NPS Summer Jobs**, then answer the following questions.

    b. Which tools will you use to find the National Park Service Web site?

    c. How might you let your friend know about this Web site?

    d. You have found a few job descriptions that interest you. You want to return to the Web site later. Which tool will you use to accomplish this?

    e. Your friend is meeting you at the library later to talk about possible jobs. How can you mark the jobs you're interested in so that you can show them to her later?

    f. Type **your name**, save and close NPS Summer Jobs, then exit the word processor.

Independent Challenge 4

Find a topic that interests you. It can be a passion you've always had, something you saw on the Internet, or an assignment you've been given in one of your classes. (*Note*: You can print or post this assignment. Please check with your instructor for assignment submission instructions.)

a. Use a subject guide to find Web sites about your topic.
b. Explore the links in the subject guide to find a tertiary source, a secondary source, and a primary source.
c. Open a document in a word processor, save it as **My Topic**, then summarize the information in each of your sources and explain why you consider them primary, secondary, and so on.
d. Bookmark the three sources and use the screen capture tool of your choice to capture the pages showing the bookmarks you have created. Paste the screen shot images into your document.
e. Go to one of the sites and use the online highlighting tool of your choice to highlight information you want to use in your research.
f. Use the screen capture tool of your choice to capture one of the highlighted pages. Paste the screen shot into your document.
g. Use the Web search engine of your choice to find a book about your topic.
h. Use a bibliography generator to create a citation for the book in MLA format. Copy and paste the text of the citation into your document.
i. Type **your name**, save and close My Topic, then exit the word processor.

Visual Workshop

Starting at the Duke University Web site, www.duke.edu, use the Libraries link to locate the Web site shown in Figure A-17. (*Note*: You can print or post this assignment. Please check with your instructor for assignment submission instructions.)

    a. Click the Libraries button on the navigation bar.

    b. Click the Databases tab under Search Resources.

    c. Type **Advertising** in the Name of Database text box, then click Go.

    d. Click the Emergence of Advertising in US link.

    e. Open a document in a word processor, save it as **Search_Highlighting**, then capture the information in the steps below.

    f. Use the online highlighting tool of your choice to highlight the text on part of the page.

    g. Print the page or use the screen capture tool of your choice to capture the highlighted text, then paste it in the document.

    h. Click the Contact Us link, then click the Ask a Librarian link.

    i. According to the link, how long will it take for a librarian to answer your question by email? Print the page, type the infomation in the document, or use the screen capture tool of your choice to capture the information and then paste it in the document.

    j. What is the screen name of the librarian to whom you can send an instant message? If not included in Step i, print the page, type the infomation in the document, or use the screen capture tool of your choice to capture the information and then paste it in the document.

    k. Type **your name**, save and then close Search_Highlighting, then exit the word processor.

FIGURE A-17

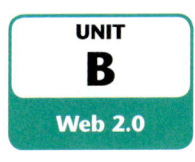

Finding Media for Projects

Files You Will Need:
No files needed

This unit assumes that students have signed up for free accounts at flickr.com and jamendo.com, and that they have a digital photograph they can upload.

The Web is full of engaging video, photos, and music, but are there restrictions on how you can use the material you find there? How do you find media you can use? What about protecting your own work? The answers to these questions lie in copyright law, a category of intellectual property law. **Intellectual property** is an idea or creation that has the potential for commercial value. Working with Web 2.0 tools brings you into contact with many types of media from many sources. Professor Ahmed has asked the class to choose a topic and create a multimedia video that requires you to find media for the project. You learn about copyright law, how to get permission to use work, how to find media that you can use, and how to protect your own work.

OBJECTIVES

Understand copyright

Use Creative Commons

Find images

Find video

Find music

Obtain permission and credit sources

Understand terms of use

Post your files online

Protect the rights to your work

UNIT B
Web 2.0

Understanding Copyright

Copyright law ensures that authors get rewarded for their efforts and that society as a whole benefits from creative works. It also gives authors control over how their works can be used. Although it might not be obvious, copyright law also motivates people to create works because it provides a financial incentive to those who create and share knowledge. Professor Ahmed wants you to familiarize yourself with the basics of copyright law so you can determine if you can use protected work in your own projects.

DETAILS

Understanding copyright protection involves the following concepts:

- **The purpose of copyright and determining what is copyrightable**

    Copyright law protects authors of original works, whether those works are published or unpublished. The word **author** refers to any creator of a copyrighted work—composer, photographer, writer, graphic designer, or animator. Copyright law balances the interests of authors with the interests of the public by giving authors a monopoly on their work for a limited time, and then dissolving that monopoly by eventually allowing the work to be accessed, and presumably improved or built on, by the public. Simply put, copyright is defined as an original creative work created by a person that someone else can experience. The major components of copyright consist of:

    - *Originality*: An independent creation. It doesn't have to be unique, but it does need a small amount of creativity. For example, the worst song you've ever heard is protected, but simply posting your favorite playlist is not.
    - *Fixation*: Established in a tangible medium; this is the defining aspect of a work being copyrightable. The work exists and it can be experienced, from a full-length movie to a graphic stored for a couple of nanoseconds in computer RAM.
    - *Expression*: A person's unique *take* on an idea. The idea itself is not protected (for example, taking a photo on the beach at sunset), but the expression of that idea is (clicking the camera at a particular moment).

- **Copyright protection**

    Duration: A work acquires copyright protection *as soon as* you create it. Generally, for an individual, copyright lasts the life of the author plus 70 years. You don't have to register your work with the U.S. Copyright Office, shown in Figure B-1, but you establish your strongest legal position when you do (at the time of this printing, the cost is $35 for electronic filing).

    Your rights: Copyright law protects your work by giving you a **bundle of rights**, including the right to make copies, create a new work based on the original (known as a **derivative work**), distribute copies, and perform or display the work publicly and digitally.

- **Fair Use**

    Fair use is a built-in limitation to copyright protection that allows users to copy all or part of a copyrighted work in support of their First Amendment and other rights. You do not need to ask permission from the copyright holder for a fair use of the work. For example, you could critique a protected film or song, or parody a popular television show or celebrity. Determining whether fair use applies to your intended use of a work depends on the *purpose* of your use, the *nature* of the copyrighted work, the *amount* you want to copy, and the *effect* on the salability or value of the original work. See Table B-1.

QUICK TIP
You should assume that every text and media file on the Internet has copyright protection or protection under another category of intellectual property law.

QUICK TIP
The familiar copyright notice, "© 2013 Course Technology," is not required to show that your work is protected, but it is always a good idea to include it.

QUICK TIP
Fair use is used as the defense in many copyright infringement cases, but it is intentionally broad and always decided on a case-by-case basis.

Finding Media for Projects

FIGURE B-1: The U.S. Copyright Office Web site (www.copyright.gov)

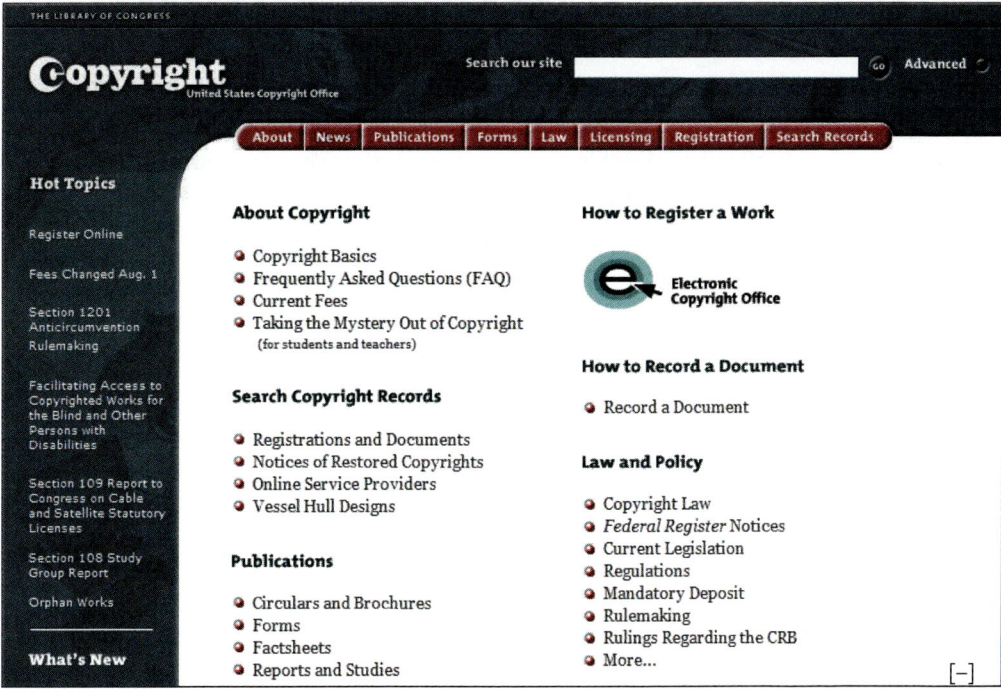

TABLE B-1: Analyzing the four factors of fair use

factor	fair use	unlikely fair use

Factor 1 Purpose and character of use	• Nonprofit educational purpose
	• Different purpose—transformative use
	  - commentary - criticism
	  - news reporting - parody
	• Research
	• Scholarship
		• Commercial—profit
		• Same purpose as original—use is not transformative
		• Entertainment (not parody)

Factor 2 Nature of copyrighted work	• Work is fact or nonfiction • Published work • Informational	• Original work has strong copyright (creative) • Unpublished work (copyright owner gets to decide if work will be made public)
Factor 3 Amount (quantity and quality)	• Small amount (relative to whole) • Portion used is not key to work	• Large amount • Heart of the work—amount used is central to work
Factor 4 Effect on the market	• No effect on the market of the original work (either positively or negatively)	• Major effect on existing or potential market • Replaces sales of original—appeals to same market • License or royalty requested was reasonable and could have been paid • Work is made available everywhere

Understanding copyright infringement and the public domain

Copyright infringement is the unauthorized use of one or more of the rights of a copyright holder. The penalty per infringement of a registered copyright can be tens of thousands of dollars. Even accidental infringement can lead to penalties. The assumptions and burdens of proof governing copyright infringement are based on civil law. Civil law does not require proof of infringement beyond a reasonable doubt. The court's assumption may be that you are guilty, and the burden of proof is on you to prove that you are not.

Works no longer protected by some form of intellectual property law are in the **public domain**; therefore, no one owns them or controls their use. You can use and modify public domain content in any way you want. The length of copyright protection has increased with each revision to the Copyright Act, so it's not always easy to determine whether a work is still protected. In the United States, nearly every work created prior to 1923 is in the public domain. Some works are never protected by copyright, such as laws and court decisions from all levels of government, and federal government documents and Web sites.

Finding Media for Projects

Using Creative Commons

UNIT B — Web 2.0

Under copyright law, the copyright owner automatically retains all rights to his or her work. Therefore, it can be difficult to make the work available to others without individually granting permission and that, of course, may not often be a feasible option. However, **Creative Commons (CC)** licensing offers an easy way to assign copyright to your work. CC licenses let creators decide which rights they want to retain while allowing others to use the work under certain conditions that the owner selects. As an owner, you can choose the type of license you want: You can require simple attribution for your work, restrict its commercial use, or not allow derivative use. As a user, you can download work confident that the owner's intentions for use are clear. Professor Ahmed has mentioned Creative Commons as an important tool that builds on the traditional copyright model. She asks you to explore the Creative Commons Web site to learn more about how to assign a CC license to your own work and how to find works that have certain CC licenses applied to them.

STEPS

1. **Go to www.creativecommons.org in your browser**
   The Creative Commons Web site opens, as shown in Figure B-2. Here you can assign a CC license to your work or search for other works that have CC licenses. You want to learn more about CC license types.

2. **Click License on the right side of the page, read the intro paragraph, click the information icon ⓘ for the Yes options in the questions, then read the definitions**
   Creative Commons provides an easy guide for users to help you select a license. Next, you view detailed explanations about the various license possibilities.

3. **In the middle section on the right, click View an explanation of all our licenses, compare your screen to Figure B-3, then scroll down to read the descriptions**
   Each license has a unique icon and outlines the conditions under which users can use the content. Note that the least restrictive license, Attribution, requires that the user give you credit, but can change and manipulate the work fully. The most restrictive license, Attribution Non-Commercial No Derivatives, allows users to redistribute the work, but they cannot profit from its use or change it.

4. **Scroll back to the top of the page, then at the top of the right section, click Find licensed works**
   The Creative Commons Search page opens. In the green section at the top of the page, you can type a search term and select options to retrieve files that the owner has allowed for commercial and derivative use. Beneath the search section are the search engines and sites you can search.

5. **At the top of the page, type coral in the Search text box, make sure that both check boxes are selected, then click Yahoo! (Web)**
   Links to sites that match both the search term and CC license options appear in the Yahoo! search results, as shown in Figure B-4. You can click another search engine or site to search using the same criteria. Note that the search results include work with *any* CC license; be sure to check the specific license to ensure you can use it the way you need.

6. **Click a few links to view the sites, then read any licensing information, if available**

QUICK TIP
Once you designate your work to be in the public domain or assign it an **open access license** (such as a CC license) you cannot take it back or change it to a more restrictive license.

TROUBLE
Creative Commons cannot absolutely guarantee that the search results will have a CC license; always verify a file's license before you download it especially for commercial use.

Finding Media for Projects

FIGURE B-2: The Creative Commons home page

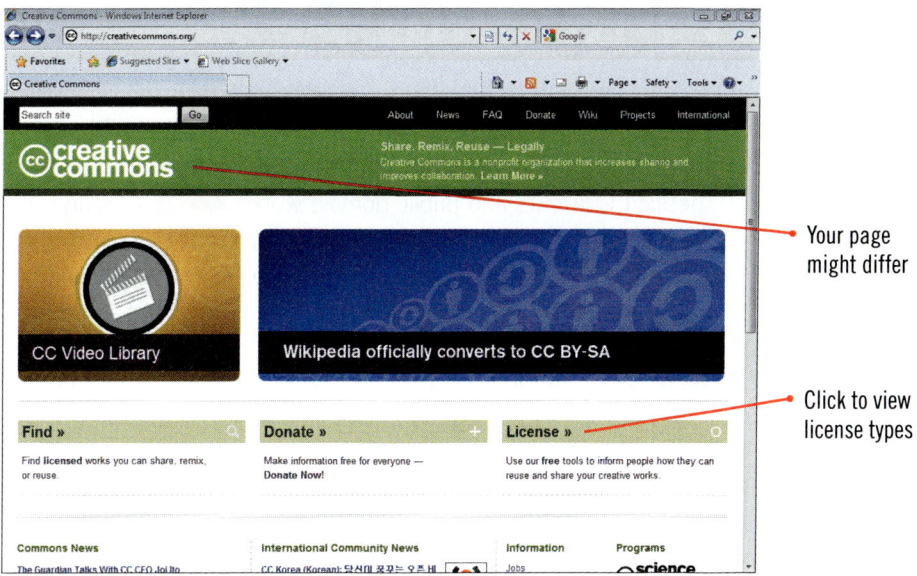

FIGURE B-3: Viewing Creative Commons license descriptions

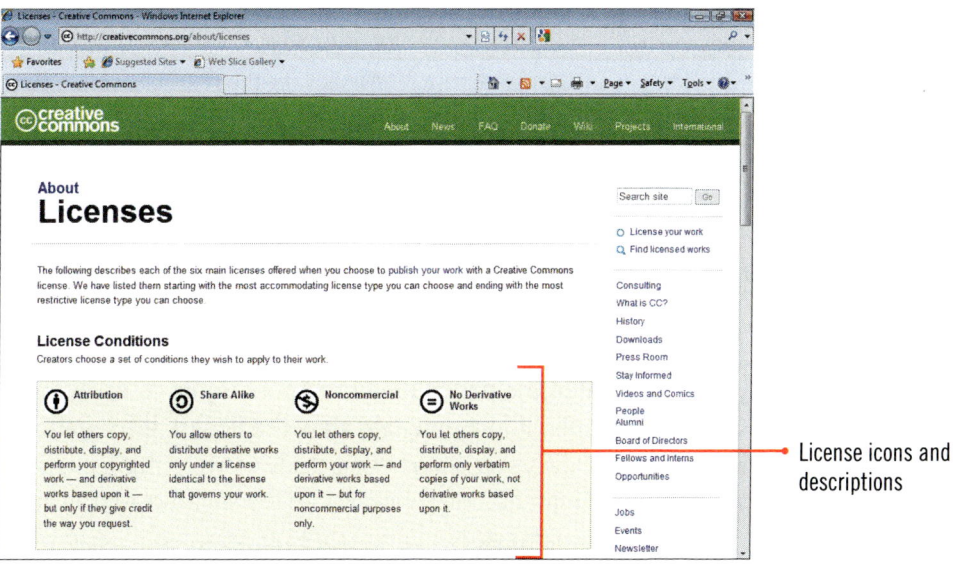

FIGURE B-4: Viewing Creative Commons search results on Yahoo!

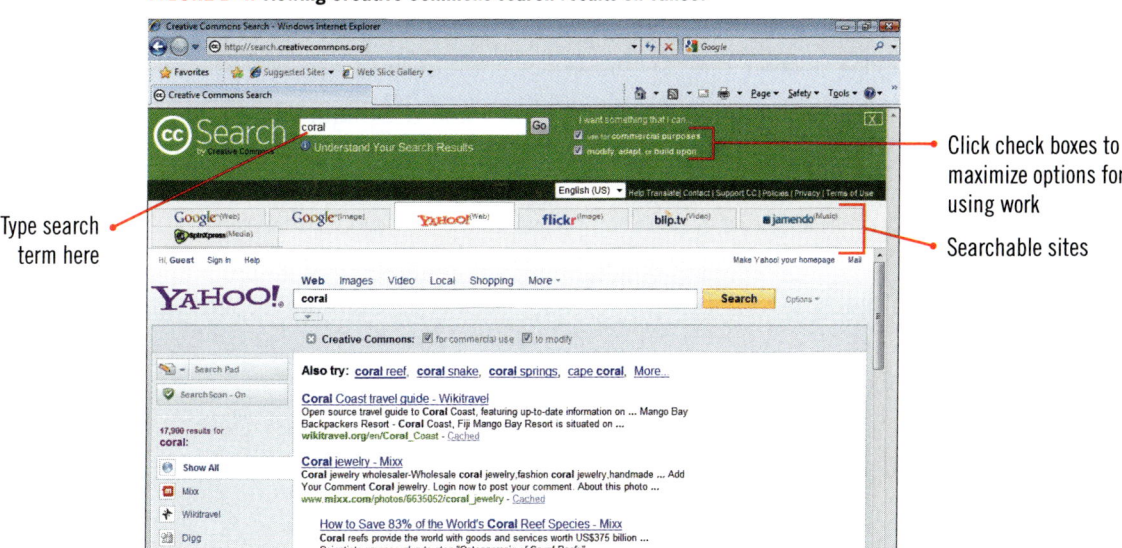

UNIT
B
Web 2.0

Finding Images

You can search for photos to use in your project using a standard search engine, but that can be time-consuming and ineffective. Fortunately, you can search some photo-sharing sites where users post CC-licensed or public domain content. Once you sign up for a free account at flickr.com, you can easily search millions of photos for specific CC licenses and public domain works. Although there are many photo-sharing sites, Professor Ahmed asks that you focus your efforts first on flickr.com. You search for CC attribution-only content and then view public domain content posted by libraries from around the world.

STEPS

QUICK TIP
Many sites offer additional services, such as uploading or downloading, only after you sign up for an account.

1. **Go to www.flickr.com in your browser, then sign in to your account**
   Your personal flickr page opens, showing your **photostream** (photos you've uploaded), contacts, and groups, if you have any.

2. **Click the Explore list arrow on the top navigation bar, click Creative Commons, compare your screen to Figure B-5, then scroll down to view each license type**
   Photos posted with a CC license are broken out by the type of license. Note the large number of photos currently posted under each license. To search for photos with a specific CC license, you open a search page for that type.

QUICK TIP
You can click the browse popular tags link beneath the Search text box to view a **tag cloud**, a type of weighted list that shows user-generated tags in different sizes based on their popularity.

3. **Under Attribution License, click See more**
   The Attribution-only CC license page opens, showing the 100 most recently uploaded photos. You can search for additional photos with this license.

4. **Type coral in the Search text box, click Search, click any thumbnail in the search results, then scroll to the Additional heading section on the right side of the page**
   The photo page contains information about the photographer and his or her photostream, tags, and copyright information, as shown in Figure B-6. To download the photo, you can click the All Sizes button above the photo, then select the size you want. You decide to confirm the copyright license assigned to the photo. To see exactly how you can use the work, you view the license.

5. **On the right side of the page, open the Some rights reserved link under Additional Information to open it in a new tab, view the license information, then close the tab**
   Creative Commons licenses are always "Some rights reserved." The terms "All rights reserved" (the same as the © symbol) and "Some rights reserved" are used in compliance with an international copyright treaty.

6. **Scroll to the bottom of the page, in the Explore section, click The Commons, then view the samples on the page**
   The Commons hosts thousands of public domain photos from libraries and institutions around the world. These photos are legally identified as having "no known copyright restriction." You want to see a list of the specific institutions currently participating in The Commons.

QUICK TIP
George Eastman invented roll film and founded the Eastman Kodak Company, which, in addition to supplying the world's film for most of the twentieth century, created the digital camera in 1975.

7. **Scroll to the icon block on the right side of the page, click Rights Statement, scroll down to Participating Institutions, then compare your screen to Figure B-7**
   The list includes links to some of the largest digitized collections, such as the Library of Congress, New York City Public Library, and the George Eastman House. To view individual terms of use, click the Rights Statement for an institution that interests you.

8. **Scroll to the top of the page, then click Sign Out in the upper-right corner**

Finding Media for Projects

FIGURE B-5: Viewing CC-licensed photos on flickr

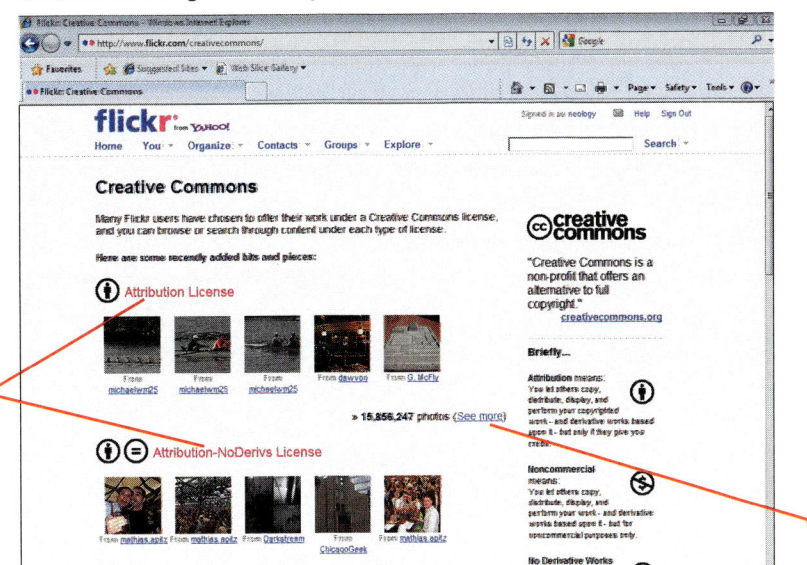

Photos broken out by license type; your thumbnails and number of photos will differ

Click to view photos with specific license

FIGURE B-6: Viewing flickr photo details

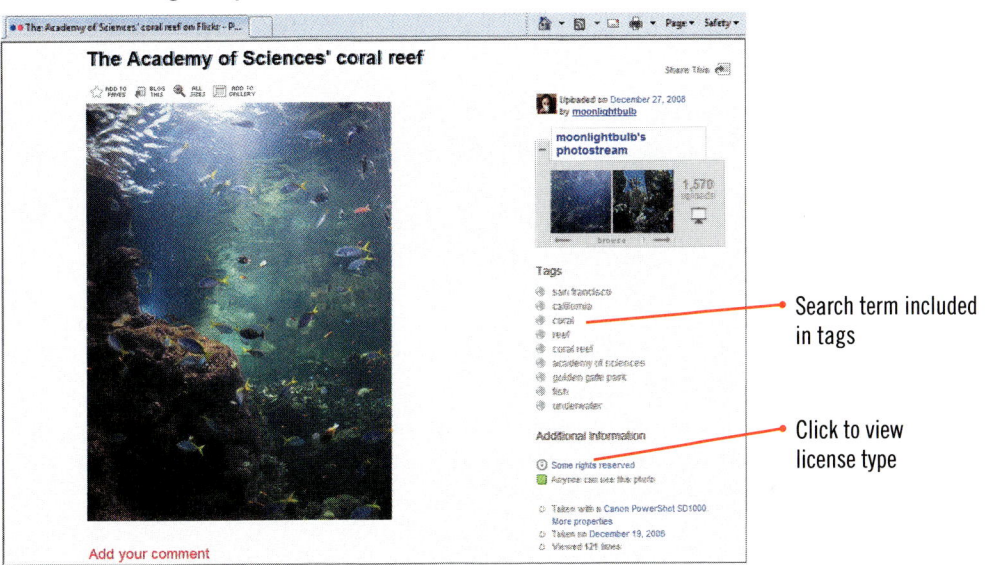

Search term included in tags

Click to view license type

FIGURE B-7: Partial list of organizations belonging to The Commons

Finding Media for Projects   29

UNIT B
Web 2.0

Finding Video

You can search for CC-licensed videos on flickr just as you search for photos. However, Web sites like YouTube or Hulu prohibit you from downloading video. Some Web sites have catalogued public domain and open access collections of classic movies, commercials, TV shows, and so on. Internet Archive, a non-profit organization, works with the Library of Congress and other private and public collections to provide free access to researchers, historians, scholars, and the general public. The site houses various media, and is well known for its collection of usable content. 🎨 Professor Ahmed has asked you to find video you can use for multimedia projects on the history of television advertising. You search the Internet Archive for classic TV commercials you will later edit in a video-editing program.

STEPS

QUICK TIP
The unique Wayback Machine allows you to enter a URL and see a list of cached versions of the site going back to when it first established a presence on the Web.

1. **Go to www.archive.org in your browser**
   Samples from various collections appear on the home page, as shown in Figure B-8.

2. **Scroll down the page, click a Curator's Choice selection in any media to view it, then click Home at the top of the page**
   You're interested in video, so you search moving images.

TROUBLE
If Prelinger Archives is not available under Moving Images, just click Moving Images.

3. **Type classic commercials in the Search text box, click the All Media Types list arrow, click Prelinger Archives, then click Go!**
   Movies matching the search criteria appear, as shown in Figure B-9. Options on the right side of the screen allow you to further sort, group, or refine your search. If necessary, use earbuds or headphones if you are in a computer lab or other public place.

4. **Scroll down, click Classic Television Commercials (Part VIII), then compare your screen to Figure B-10**
   The movie page provides options for viewing or downloading the movie (stream or download). **Streaming media** plays as your browser downloads the file. You can also confirm a movie's copyright status and read reviews. You watch the movie.

QUICK TIP
To download a file, right-click the link, then click Save Target As or Save Link As (Win), or press and hold the mouse button over the link, then click Save Linked File As (Mac).

5. **Click the green Click to play video button to play the movie, then watch at least three commercials**

6. **Click the Pause button in the player or click the Back button in your browser to stop the movie**

Understanding the right of publicity and right of privacy

The **right of publicity** protects against the use of an individual's likeness for commercial advantage. This right is asserted by celebrities who are in a position to lose financially from the unauthorized use of their identities. Identity is defined as their name, voice, and likeness. The **right of privacy** protects all of us from interference with our right to be left alone and to protect ourselves from unwarranted publicity. You should obtain permission, known as a **model release**, when you use photos or video for commercial purposes and the individual is recognizable. Children (legal minors) require a separate model release signed by their parent or guardian. As a *general rule*, if both you and the subject are in a public place, a model release may not be required for non-commercial use. Be aware that even if an image or movie is in the public domain for copyright purposes, its use may still be protected by right of publicity.

Finding Media for Projects

FIGURE B-8: The Internet Archive Web site

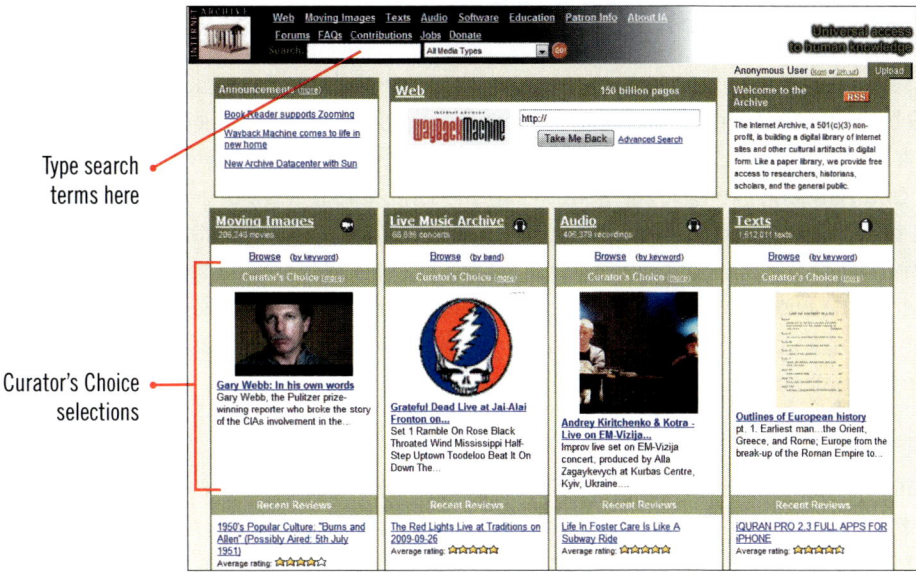

FIGURE B-9: Search results for the Prelinger Archives

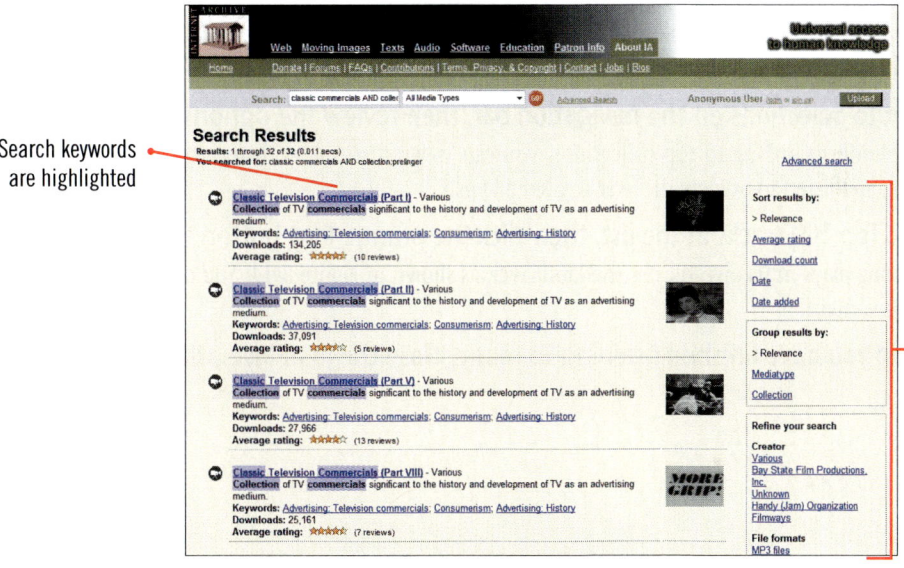

FIGURE B-10: Viewing individual movie information

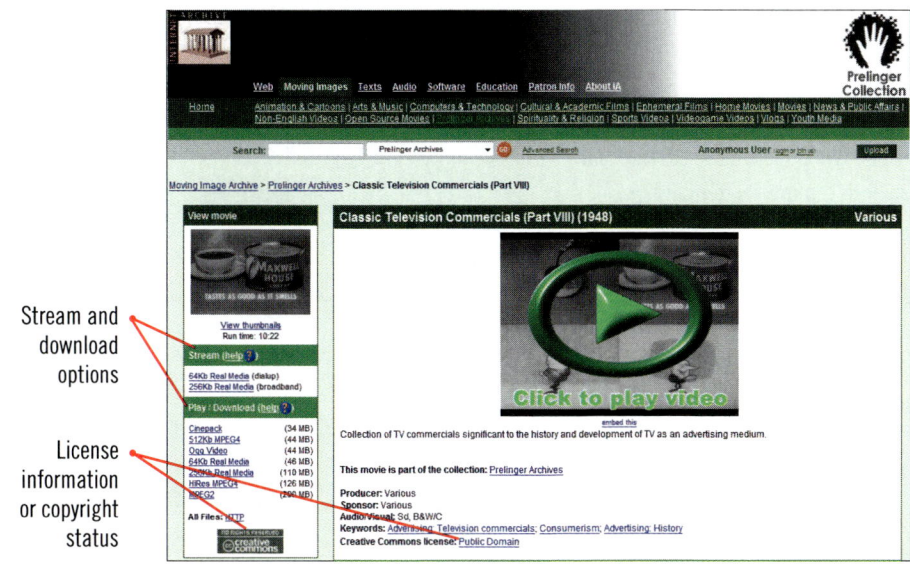

Finding Media for Projects

UNIT B
Web 2.0

Finding Music

You can search for CC-licensed music on the Internet Archive Web site the same way you search for video. Other Web sites that support CC licensing contain full songs or albums, sound loops, and sound effects. You may think that once you purchase a song legally, you have the right to do anything you want with it. That isn't the case. Although you have the right to play the song, give it away, or even destroy it, you can only do these things under your rights of personal use. When you post a song on the Internet improperly, you violate the right of the copyright owner to publicly perform his or her work. To properly post a song, you need permission (a license) to use the work. For your project, you'd like to have a full-length song playing in the background. Professor Ahmed suggests you check out music that has CC licensing. You start your search at jamendo.com.

STEPS

1. **Go to www.jamendo.com, then click the take a tour button in the upper-right corner of the page**

   Links to popular albums and tracks appear on the home page, as shown in Figure B-12.

2. **Click jamendo in the upper-left corner to return to the home page, click Please login! in the upper-right corner, then sign in to your account**

   The welcome page opens for members, as shown in Figure B-13. Here you can access additional sharing options. First you want to check out the top tracks.

3. **Point to Selections on the navigation bar, then review the options in the list**

   In addition to linking to top collections, you can view artists' blogs, listen to streaming radio of jamendo music, and listen to or view the user-created playlists.

TROUBLE
If you receive a blocked pop-up warning, click Temporarily Allow Pop-Ups.

4. **Click Top 100 tracks in the list, then click the orange Play button to listen to a song**

   The song plays in its own player, the JamPlayer, as shown in Figure B-14. You can listen to or download any of this content.

QUICK TIP
To download a song, click the down arrow button or download link, then click Download.

5. **When you have finished listening to music, close the JamPlayer, then log out**

Creating music collaboratively online

Many music and sound Web sites support Creative Commons and encourage users to submit and create remixes, samples, and **mashups** (a combination of media). Two popular sites, ccMixter and OWL Multimedia, are defined by their community relationships. Open your browser, then navigate to www.ccmixter.org. To upload music, sign up for a free account. You can listen to and download editors' picks, remixes, samples, a cappella songs, and so on. All content is licensed with a CC Noncommercial Sampling Plus 1.0 license, shown in Figure B-11. To find music that matches parts of a song similar to one you want, navigate to www.owlmm.com. Here you can open your song from your computer, locate your favorite passage, and then direct OWL to find online songs based on year, genre, and CC license.

FIGURE B-11: CC Sampling license

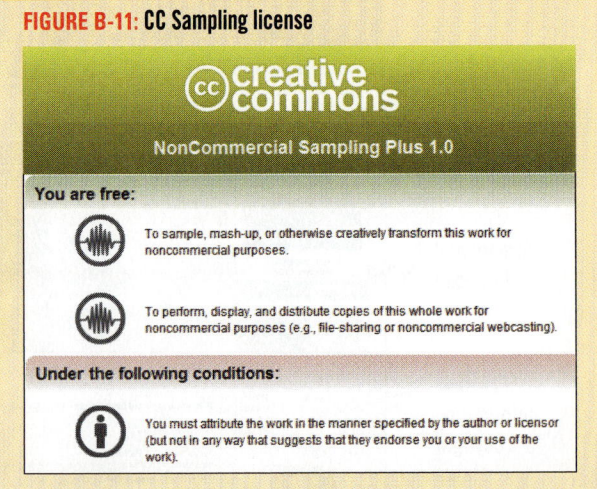

Finding Media for Projects

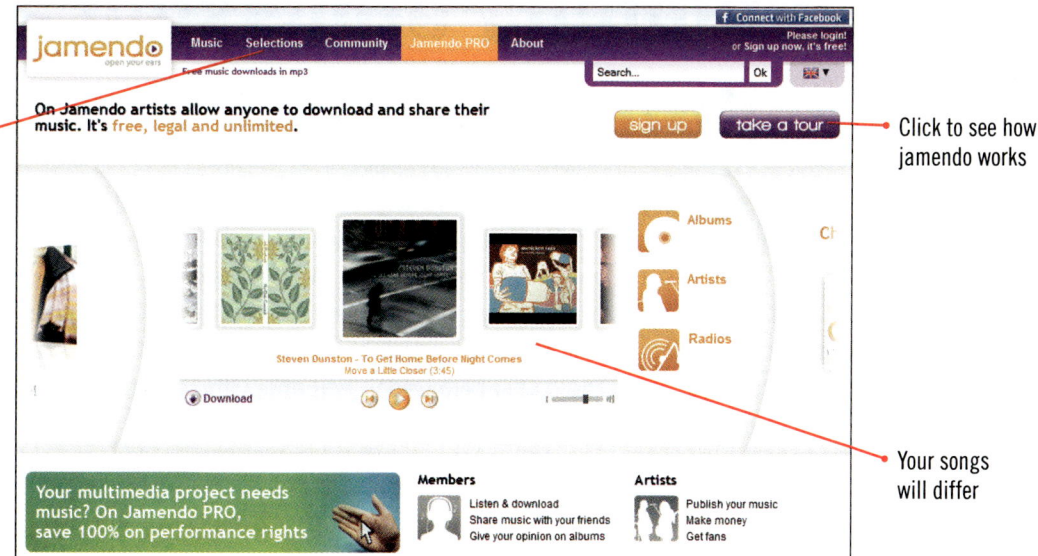

FIGURE B-12: The jamendo.com music home page

FIGURE B-13: Viewing the jamendo member welcome page

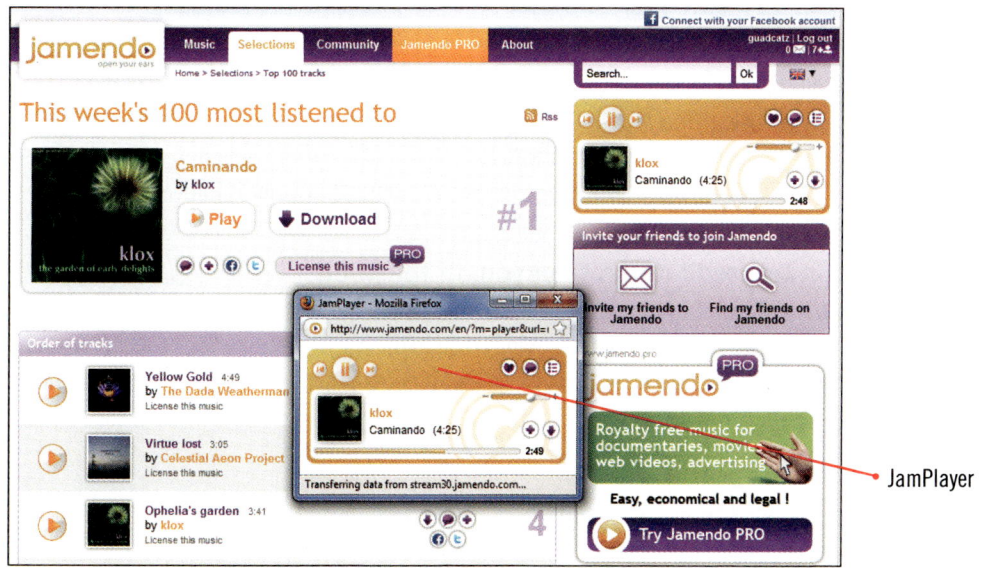

FIGURE B-14: Listening to a song on jamendo

Finding Media for Projects

Obtaining Permission and Crediting Sources

UNIT B — Web 2.0

Many well-intended users of protected content get confused between getting permission to use a work and crediting the creator of the work. If you use a work improperly, that is, you do not follow the conditions set forth in the license or do not have permission to use a work, you can set yourself up for unpleasant legal action. Professor Ahmed wants you to enrich your projects with great online content while significantly minimizing the risk of a legal action being brought against you. To acquire the expert skills you'll need to find content and gather permissions, you review the specifics for obtaining permission and attributing work.

DETAILS

Consider the following when determining permissions and attribution:

- **Understanding permissions**

  Thousands of copyright holders of various media are committed to sharing their content outright. Many simply expect that you ask permission—which is exactly within their legal rights. Still others might require that you pay a fee, which might be surprisingly within your price range or well worth the value you are receiving.

  > **QUICK TIP**
  > The fee paid to a musician for the right to play their song is known as a **royalty**.

- **How do I obtain permission?**

  Your permissions request should include specifics about what you want to use (text, photographs, music, trademarks, merchandise, and so on) and how you want to use it (school paper, personal Web site, book illustration, art piece). Obviously, getting permission from an amateur photographer whose work you found on a photo-sharing Web site might be easier than getting permission from a large music publisher. How you want to use the work determines the level and scope of permissions you need to secure; getting permission to stage a school play differs from permission to cover a Top 40 song in your debut CD. The fundamentals, however, are the same. See the sample request shown in Figure B-15. Your request should contain the following:
  - Your full name, addresses, and complete contact information.
  - A specific description of your intended use; sometimes including a sketch, storyboard, or link to a Web site is helpful.
  - A signature line for the copyright holder.
  - A target date when you would like the copyright holder to respond; this can be important if you're working under a deadline.

  See Table B-2 for sources to contact to obtain permission to use a work.

  > **QUICK TIP**
  > Getting permission to use multimedia works can be complicated because each component—text, music, the actual recording, graphics, video, and animation—requires its own permission.

- **Silence is not always golden**

  Not surprisingly, your assumption should be that you do not have permission to use a work until you actually receive it. You absolutely cannot insert language in your permission letter such as "If I do not hear back from you within one month I will assume you have given me permission to use the work." There is no time limit for a copyright owner to write back. A copyright owner is under no obligation to respond to a request; silence means "No."

- **Giving credit doesn't get you off the hook**

  It is important to understand that attribution, although a great standard practice, is never a defense against infringement. In other words, giving credit to the copyright holder of a song or photo indicates that you are not trying to claim the work as your own, but it doesn't mean you are using the work properly, with permission.

Finding Media for Projects

FIGURE B-15: Sample permissions request

My Name
Contact Information

Date
Name
Address of copyright holder

Dear *Name of Copyright Holder,*

I am *a student or other description*. I would like permission to use *description of work and location* for the following purpose: *description of purpose: how, where, frequency, and modification.*

Please complete the information at the bottom of this page and return the original to me in the enclosed stamped envelope. I have also enclosed a copy for your records.

If you are not the copyright holder of this material, please let me know. Thank you for your time and assistance.

Sincerely,
My Signature
My Printed Name

_____

I grant permission for the use of the above material.

Signature_____ Date_____
Credit line: _____

TABLE B-2: Sources to contact to obtain permission for a multimedia work

media	possible contacts
print and Web text	Writer, publisher, Web site owner; if image is of a celebrity, right of publicity protection may be involved
music and audio	Composer, songwriter, lyricist, record label; if public performance, ASCAP or BMI licensing organizations
film, animation, and video	Production company, distributor, actors, director, producer, screenwriter
still images and art	Creator, museum, gallery; if printed image, publisher

Finding Media for Projects

UNIT B
Web 2.0

Understanding Terms of Use

The rules that Web site owners use to establish use of their work are known as **terms of use**. Sometimes, creators eager to share their work may post media without disclosing the license or copyright status of a work and expect you to figure out how you can use it by reading the Web site's terms of use. A large company will have lawyers draft the language, a small business or personal site may make it up as they go. When looking for copyright information on a Web site, you soon learn that there is no universal standard on where terms of use appear or how informative they are. With the skills you learn in Professor Ahmed's class, you hope to visit many sites that offer material for others to use. To make sure you fully understand your rights and the Web site owner's rights, you learn more about terms of use.

DETAILS

Learning how to find and negotiate terms of use involves the following:

- **Locating terms of use**

    While Web designers learn how to build Web sites and include basics such as contact information, there are no clear standards for what a terms of use page should look like or even where in the site it should be located. When searching for terms of use in a Web site, look for links such as Terms, Terms of Use, Copyright, FAQ, About Me, About Us, Use, Usage, Contact Us, and similar words. Sometimes you will even need to open a photo or image page before reaching copyright information.

- **Using terms of use**

    > **QUICK TIP**
    > Terms of use cannot include illegal or absurd conditions.

    The terms of use agreement is a contract between you and the Web site. As soon as you open a page on a Web site, you enter into a legal agreement: you agree to the terms posted on the site. This is true even if you never read the terms or don't understand them. If you don't agree with the terms, don't use the site.

    Figure B-16 shows sample terms of use. Ideally, the terms should clearly identify the copyright status or licensing of the material and how users can use it, as the Open Clip Art Library and EMOL terms state in the figure. Note that a site offering public domain media can still request that you credit them in your projects, as NOAA does in the figure. They're not asserting ownership of the material, but they can request attribution for *providing* the material.

    Be wary of Web sites that erroneously assert copyright ownership over public domain materials simply because they have placed them in their collection. On the other hand, large stock image companies may charge for digitizing and creating high-resolution copies of public domain images.

    Even when terms of use are clearly stated on a site, some users interpret them differently, loosely, or not at all. That is often because the terms include common words such as personal, educational, commercial, internal, corporate, nonprofit, free, and public domain, and those words mean different things to different people. For instance, most people assume "personal use" refers to one's private, not professional life. To some people, the definition of "educational use" might mean use by students and teachers in elementary and high school classes only, whereas to others it might indicate the instructor can use a work but students cannot.

Finding Media for Projects

FIGURE B-16: Viewing terms of use

Restrictions for Using NOAA Images

Most NOAA photos and slides are in the public domain and **CANNOT** be copyrighted. There is no fee for downloading any images on the NOAA Photo Library. Educational use is encouraged as the primary goal of the NOAA Photo Library is to help all understand our oceans and atmosphere so as to be better stewards of our environment for future generations.

A few photos in the NOAA Photo Library that are known to have copyright restrictions are so noted in the caption information associated with those images.

Credit **MUST** be given to the National Oceanic and Atmospheric Administration/Department of Commerce. Where a photographer is noted, please credit the photographer and his/her affiliated organization as well.

National Oceanic & Atmospheric Administration (NOAA) – www.noaa.gov

---

Free Sound Samples

Sample some of our stereo recorded MP3 sound effects and flash sound samples

From our 892 Sound Effects Download - Personal and Commercial Use Sounds

www.a1freesoundeffects.com

What limitations are there in how I can use the clipart?

There are no limitations, you can do whatever you wish with it.

We select the Public Domain for the clipart in order to provide maximum flexibility and ease of use to the user. You can put the clipart into your own drawings without any affect on the copyright or license of your work. There are no requirements to include attribution of the clipartist. You can edit and modify the clipart as you wish and redistribute it under your own terms.

Open Clip Art Library – www.openclipart.org

Download Free Movies

All of the public domain movies are absolutely free to watch and download. These free movies are also legal to transfer to a mobile player or PC. No registration, fees or log in is required to watch or download these movies and videos.

Duplicate and distribute them, or transfer the movies to mobile devices like iPods, iPhones and other video, smart and cell phones.

Entertainment Magazine Online – www.emol.org/movies

Finding Media for Projects

UNIT B
Web 2.0

Posting Your Files Online

Posting your work online on a personal photo-sharing site is a simple upload procedure. When you upload content you want to share, the process is a bit more complicated. You need to verify that you can legally share the work. In addition, each site has its own uploading process. Professor Ahmed suggests you examine the uploading process for some of the sites you visited in this unit.

STEPS

QUICK TIP
In addition to using the Web site's uploading feature, you can download a desktop uploader for your operating system.

TROUBLE
There are **very** serious legal consequences to assigning a Creative Commons license to copyright-protected work. If you did not create a work, do not assign a CC license to it.

QUICK TIP
The demo movie is mostly silent until halfway through.

1. **Go to www.flickr.com, sign in to your account, scroll to the bottom navigation bar to the right of You, click Upload, then follow the steps to upload a photo**
   To view the downloader page, scroll to the Help navigation bar on the bottom of the page, then click Tools.

2. **Add a description, click Save, then when you see your uploaded photo, click the copyright symbol ©**
   The Set a license for this photo page opens, as shown in Figure B-17. Here you can select a CC license. The default license is the standard one: you keep all your rights, so you must select a CC license if you want to share your work.

3. **Select the license of your choice, then click Save**
   Your photo is now shared and can be used by others in the way you designated. Next, you learn about uploading and licensing music.

4. **Navigate to www.jamendo.com, sign in to your account, point to Music on the top navigation bar, then click Upload your music**
   The Upload your album page appears, as shown in Figure B-18. Music is more complicated than still images, so you watch the demo movie. You will not upload music in this lesson.

5. **Click the orange Play button to watch the demo movie**

6. **When you have finished watching the movie, close your browser**

Fair use examples

You must weigh each factor of fair use to determine whether your use is fair. The examples below illustrate fair use analysis.

facts	factor 1 purpose	factor 2 nature	factor 3 amount	factor 4 effect	possible ruling
Scan and digitally alter a protected photo to use in an animated Web ad	Animation ad is for commercial use	The source photo is creative work	The entire photo is copied	Ad directly affects market for photo	✘ NOT FAIR USE
	✘ weighs against fair use	✘ weighs against fair use	✘ weighs against fair use	✘ weighs against fair use	
Compare authenticity of reality television shows for class	Nonprofit use (educational)	TV snippets are published creative works	Use short (<1 min) snippets incidental to episode	Project does not affect market for shows	✓ FAIR USE
	✓ weighs for fair use	✘ weighs against fair use	✓ weighs for fair use	✓ weighs for fair use	

Finding Media for Projects

FIGURE B-17: Setting a CC license on flickr

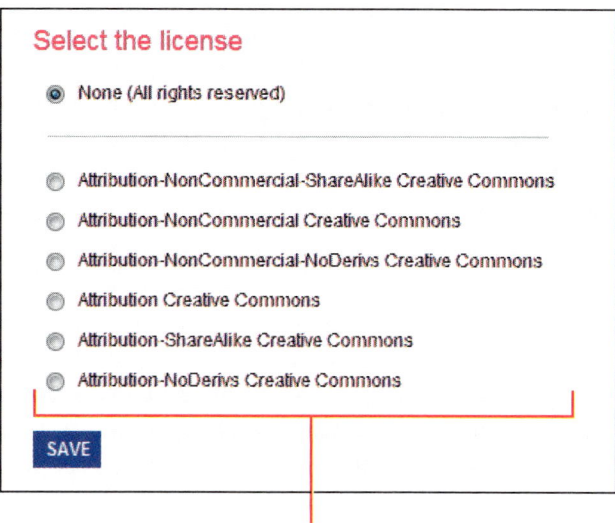

Select a CC license or keep None for full rights

FIGURE B-18: Viewing uploading options on jamendo.com

Point to Music to select upload music option

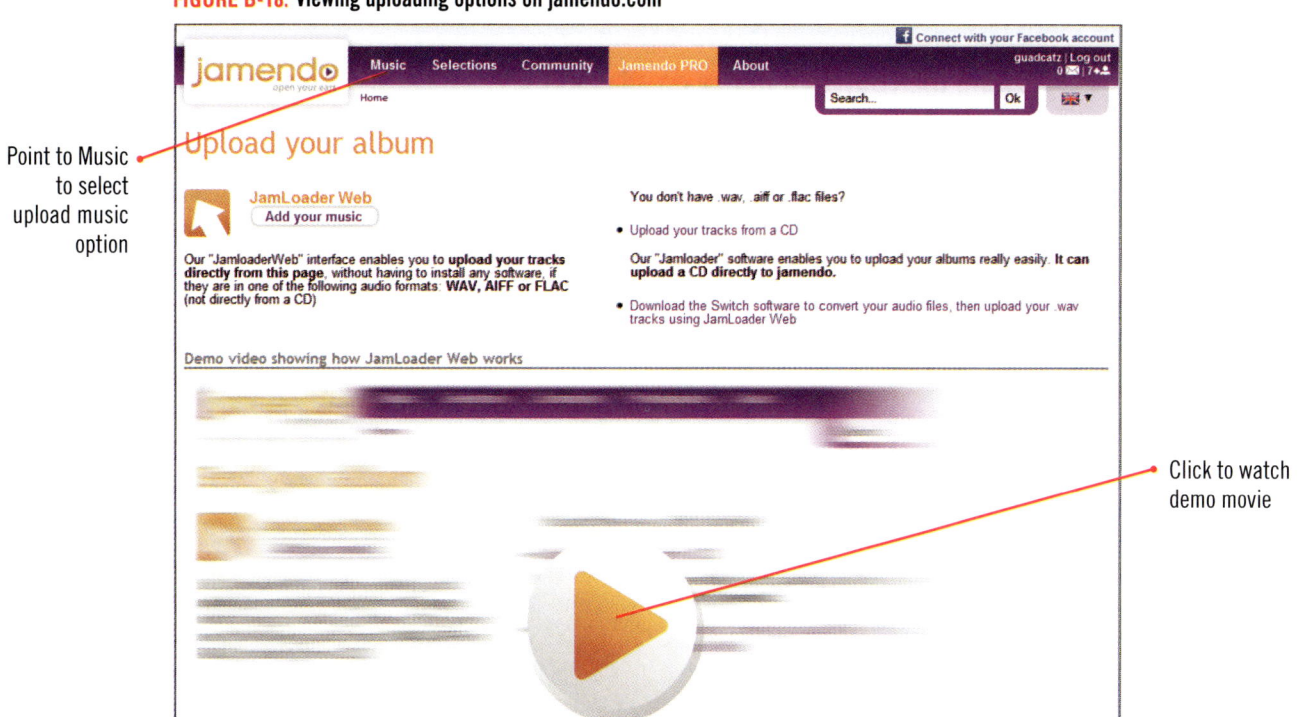

Click to watch demo movie

Finding Media for Projects

UNIT B Web 2.0

Protecting the Rights to Your Work

In reality, you may not think twice about downloading work you want to use, but the thought of someone using something you created—and possibly profiting from it—might make you reconsider. To protect your own work, you can register a work with the Copyright Office, include a copyright notice with your work, or insert a digital watermark in an image or file. You expect to be producing a lot of creative work in Professor Ahmed's class and throughout your college career. To ensure you know how to protect it, you learn more about copyright registration, the copyright notice, and digital watermarks.

DETAILS

Protecting your own work involves the following:

- **Registering your work with the Copyright Office**

    Convinced you have a work of such high value that you need to protect it with the full weight of copyright law? Register it with the Copyright Office. To register a single work or a body of work (such as the landscape photos you took in a year or the movies you created in an animation class), you fill out a form, pay a fee, and submit a copy of the work to the Copyright Office (www.copyright.gov). The registration becomes effective on the day the Copyright Office receives the package, regardless of when they send back notification to you. Figure B-19 shows the steps for registering a work at the Copyright Office.

    You gain several legal advantages by registering your work. You clearly establish yourself as the copyright owner, and if someone infringes your work, you can file suit for damages or attorneys' fees. Without registration, you can be awarded actual damages and the profit others made using your work (which usually isn't very much). But, if you register your work within three months after publication of the work or prior to an infringement of the work, you can be awarded **statutory damages** (a monetary award specifically stated in the law) and attorneys' fees (at the discretion of the court). Finally, if your work is pirated, you can prevent pirated copies from entering the United States.

- **Posting the copyright notice on all work**

    Although you've learned that you do not need to post a copyright notice, it does serve a useful purpose. When you post it, it states clearly that the work is protected by copyright. Someone who violates any of your copyrights can never claim ignorance of the law as an excuse or defense. The proper notification includes, in order, the word "Copyright" or its symbol ©, the year it obtained protection, and the name of the copyright holder, such as © 2013 Course Technology.

- **Inserting a watermark**

    QUICK TIP
    Watermarks trace their origin to thirteenth-century Italy, where a metal stamp was inserted into paper during manufacturing.

    A **digital watermark** embeds digital data into an image, audio, or video file. The data is used to identify, track, authenticate, and control the file's use. A watermark can be visible, which you can easily see in most currency, or added to a photograph in an image-editing program, as shown in Figure B-20. It can also be included with a file's metadata. **Metadata** includes information such as camera type, exposure, shutter speed, and date.

Finding Media for Projects

FIGURE B-19: Copyright Office registration information

FIGURE B-20: Samples of watermarks

Watermarks

Finding Media for Projects

Practice

Key Terms

author
bundle of rights
copyright law
copyright infringement
Creative Commons (CC)
derivative work

digital watermark
fair use
intellectual property
mashups
metadata
model release

open access license
photostream
public domain
right of privacy
right of publicity

royalty
statutory damages
streaming media
tag cloud
terms of use

Unit Review

1. Copyright law is a category of what broad area of law?
2. Name three types of work protected by copyright.
3. At what point is a work protected by copyright?
4. Explain what Creative Commons licenses allow.
5. Give an example of when a work enters the public domain.
6. Discuss the difference between crediting authors for their work and getting permission to use a work.
7. Name three rights copyright holders have to their work.
8. Name three things you should include in a permissions letter.
9. What do you call the rules users post describing how their work can be used?
10. Why shouldn't you assign a Creative Commons license to scanned photographs you found in a box in the attic?

Fill in the best answer

1. The fee paid to copyright owners, such as artists, authors, or musicians, for the right to use their work is known as a(n) _____.
2. Creating a new work based on the original is known as _____.
3. The symbol that indicates copyright protection is _____.
4. A work established in a tangible medium meets the _____ component of copyright.
5. _____ is the unauthorized use of one or more of the rights of a copyright holder.
6. When works are no longer protected by some form of intellectual property, they are said to be in the _____.
7. The four factors courts consider as built-in limitation to copyright protection are known as _____.
8. In Creative Commons licensing, the least restrictive license would require _____.
9. The protection against someone using a celebrity's likeness is known as _____.
10. To ensure you can use an image of a person in a commercial work, you should obtain a written _____.

Select the best answer from the list of choices.

1. Which of the following would not be an example of a derivative work made from a short story?
   a. A film based on the story.
   b. A review of the short story.
   c. A music video based on the story.
   d. A TV show based on the story.
2. What is our right to be left alone known as?
   a. Right of publicity.
   b. Copyright infringement.
   c. Right of privacy.
   d. Our bundle of rights.
3. Which of the following rights is not controlled by the copyright holder?
   a. Critiquing the work.
   b. Making a copy of the work.
   c. Distributing the work.
   d. Publicly performing the work.
4. After you create a work, what must you do before you can insert words stating that your work is protected by copyright?
   a. Nothing.
   b. Post the work on a Web site.
   c. Register the work with the Copyright Office.
   d. Distribute the work.
5. Which of the following represents a minimum requirement for copyright protection?
   a. "Creativity" as defined by Congress.
   b. New and unique.
   c. The number of views a work gets on the Web.
   d. A small amount of creativity.
6. Which of the following best describes Creative Commons licensing?
   a. Increasing copyright protection.
   b. Repressing copyright protection.
   c. Infringing copyright.
   d. Providing an alternative to copyright.
7. What should you assume when you see the words "no known copyright restriction"?
   a. The work is protected.
   b. That you should get written permission to use the work.
   c. The work is in the public domain.
   d. The words are an alternative to copyright.

Independent Challenge 1

You were hired to design a Web site for a local skateboard shop. The owners would like some unique sounds for the button rollovers, and played for you some sounds they like. You have no idea where they got them, so you'll search a couple of sound Web sites for public domain or open access files and verify their terms of use. (*Note*: To download files, you must set up an account.) You can print or post this assignment. Please check with your instructor for assignment submission instructions.

   a. Go to www.looperman.com.
   b. Locate the terms of use or description of the copyright status of the works posted on the site, then print the page(s).
   c. Click the Loops & Samples link on the navigation bar, click the Category list arrow, select a category, then click Search For Loops.

Independent Challenge 1 (continued)

d. Listen to several loops, then select another category and listen to several loops. Download or print the page of loops you liked.
e. Navigate to www.freesound.org, locate the terms of use or description of the copyright status of the work, then print the page(s).
f. Return to the Home page, then in the middle pane, click the Play button to listen to the Random Sound of the Day.
g. In the right pane, scroll down, listen to two of the Most popular files (last 7 days), then listen to two sounds under Highest rated sounds.
h. In the upper-right corner of the page, type **spooky** in the Search text box, click search, then listen to several sounds. Compare your screen to Figure B-21. (*Hint*: Play several sounds at once.)
i. Download or print the page of sounds you liked, then close your browser.

FIGURE B-21

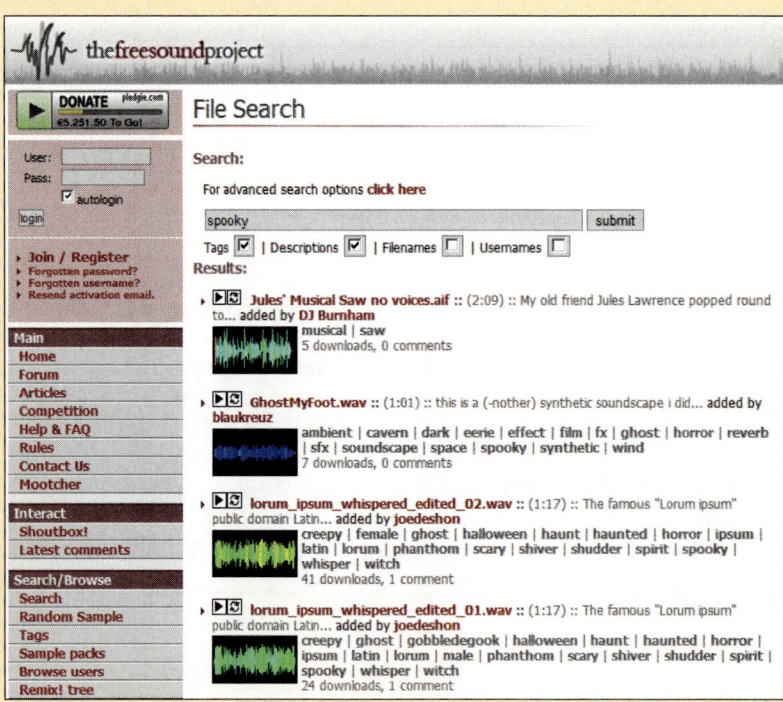

Independent Challenge 2

You have a job in the community outreach department of a local art museum. The museum is planning an exhibit on media from the Cold War to today's security scares. Your boss asks you find some vintage media from the Cold War they can play in a kiosk. You begin your search at Internet Archive. (*Note*: You can print or post this assignment. Please check with your instructor for assignment submission instructions.)

a. Go to www.archive.org.
b. Type **duck and cover** in the Search text box, click the All Media Types list arrow, click Moving Images, then click Go.
c. Click Duck and Cover – Archer Productions, Inc. in the search results, then compare your screen to Figure B-22.
d. View the movie in the format of your choice, or click View thumbnails if you are unable to watch the movie.
e. Drag the frame marker to approximately 03:45 on the timeline, then print the screen. (*Hint*: Use the screen capture tool of your choice.) Print another screen of the movie.
f. Close your browser.

Independent Challenge 2 (continued)

FIGURE B-22

Independent Challenge 3

You're helping a friend develop a blog about panoramic photography. You want to catch the interest of followers by posting several photos daily, both current and vintage photos. You want to find sites where you can be confident that the users want to their work to be used with the fewest restrictions possible. You will search a photo-sharing site known as morgueFile, where photographers post their work, and the Library of Congress, which houses over 130 million creative works, about one and one-half million of which are photographs or audio files. Much of the work is in the public domain. (*Note*: You can print or post this assignment. Please check with your instructor for assignment submission instructions.)

   a. Go to www.morguefile.com.
   b. Locate the terms of use or description of the copyright status of work posted on morgueFile. Print the page that describes the morgueFile license.
   c. Type **panorama** in the Search text box, then click Search.
   d. View several photos and different pages, then print or download the three you like best.
   e. Go to www.loc.gov, click American Memory at the top of the page, then click Go.
   f. Click Architecture, Landscape in the Browse Collections by Topic section, then click Panoramic Photographs - 1851–1991.
   g. Click Place in the Browse Collection by section, click the letter of your state, then click a city.
   h. Click Gallery at the bottom of the page in the Display section to view thumbnails.
   i. Click a thumbnail, view the copyright information, then click the photo to view it in a large version. Print or download a few photos that you like.
   j. Close your browser.

Independent Challenge 4

You can't wait to use the skills you learned in this unit to find media related to your favorite interests. It can be a passion you've always had, something you saw on the Internet, or an assignment you've been given in one of your classes. (*Note*: You can print or post this assignment. Please check with your instructor for assignment submission instructions.)

   a. Use the Web sites you visited in this unit to find photo, sound/music, and video files on the topic of your choice. (*Hint*: The Internet Archive also contains music.)
   b. Locate at least three files of each type and print the copyright status for the site or for the file.
   c. Use the search engine of your choice to search for **public domain music**, **public domain images**, and **public domain video**. Explore at least three sites for each search.
   d. Determine whether and how you can use the content, then print or download the copyright and terms of use pages for three sites.

Visual Workshop

Navigate to the Internet Archive at www.archive.org, then locate the movie shown in Figure B-23. (*Note*: You can print or post this assignment. Please check with your instructor for assignment submission instructions.)

   a. Search under Moving Images for Open Source Movies.
   b. Perform a search with the following keywords: **chroma background**.
   c. View the search results until you find the one shown in the figure.
   d. Play the movie once, drag the frame marker to 00:16 seconds, as shown in Figure B-23, then print the page.
   e. Use the skills you learned in this unit to verify that the film is in the public domain, then close your browser.

FIGURE B-23

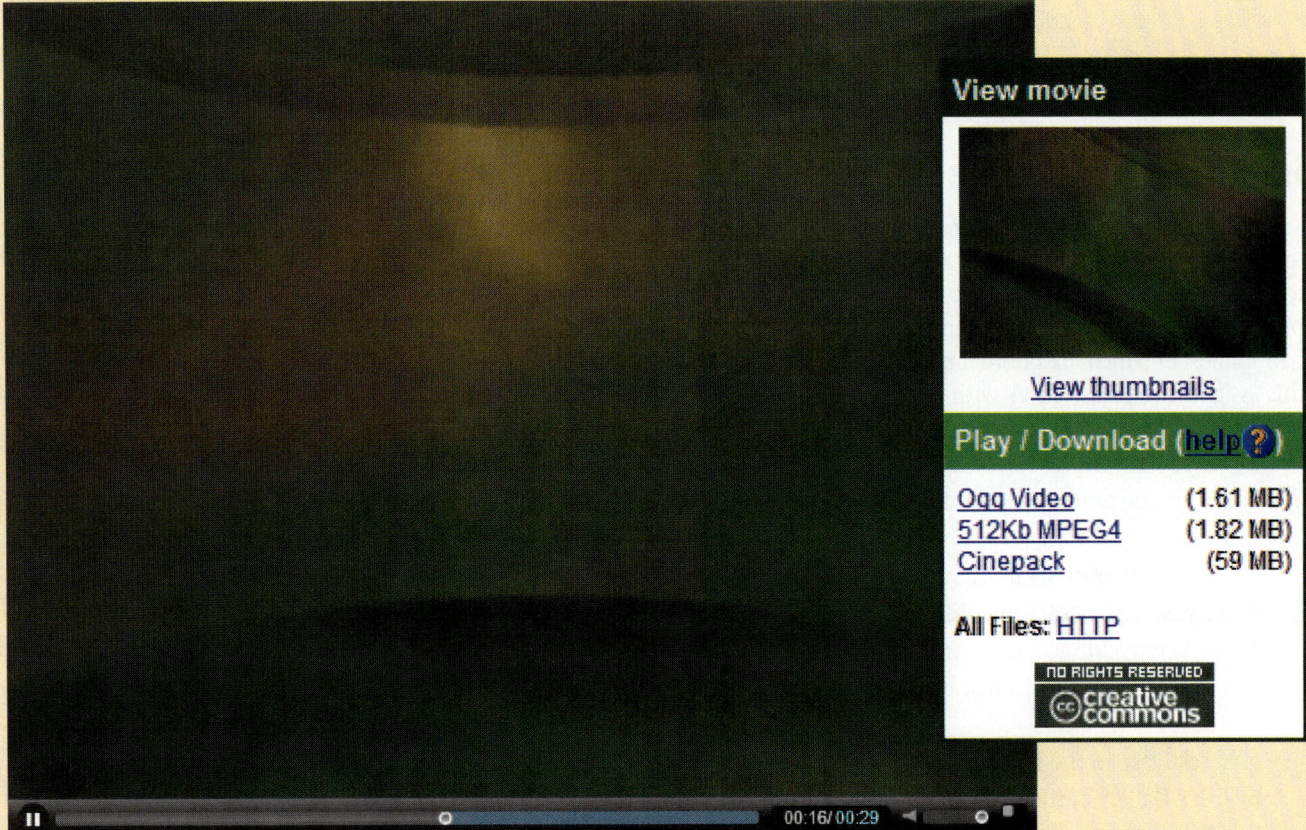

UNIT C
Web 2.0

Collaborating and Sharing Information

Files You Will Need:
No files needed

Web 2.0 technologies have changed the way businesses do business and governments govern. Businesses use the Web to get feedback from consumers on their products and services. Using this information, they can implement changes more quickly than ever before. In the new business model, "customer support" takes on a second meaning, where customers play an active role in supporting and improving products, rather than simply the passive consumer role of the past. Governments use Web 2.0 technologies to educate citizens, share data within their organizations, and provide online services that cut down on much of the bureaucracy of the past. Even private citizens have benefitted from the collaborative features of the Web. Educational institutions use these advances to provide virtual classrooms; professors use them to post assignments, lectures, and resources; students use them to work together in groups, share information, critique each other's work, and produce high-quality group projects. Professor Ahmed wants you to research the collaborative and information-sharing tools available online, and use them in a group project where you create a new product and then present it to the class using Web 2.0 technologies.

OBJECTIVES

View government Web sites
Understand business and Web 2.0
Schedule meetings
Brainstorm solutions
Use online polling
Use collaborative software
Present your work

UNIT C
Web 2.0

Viewing Government Web Sites

Governments have used the Web for years to convey information to the public and to provide online services like renewing a driver's license. However, in recent years, government's use of the Web has changed dramatically, thanks to Web 2.0 technologies. During the 2008 U.S. presidential election, the power of the Web was apparent when both parties used it to raise funds and to get out their messages on social networking and media sites. Federal, state, and local governments also use the Web to gather information, which they then use to share resources, build consensus, improve services, and make policy decisions. Your group decides that studying the ways the government uses the Web might help you develop and promote your product.

DETAILS

The following are some of the ways governments use Web 2.0 technologies:

- **Blogs and microblogs**

    Governments use **blogs** (a contraction of the words "Web" and "log") as public relations tools. Bloggers publish frequently, often daily, and have **followers** who sign up to receive updates. Figure C-1 shows the White House blog, which includes a list of the other blogs posted on the whitehouse.gov site; it also shows a blog called "Talking Trash," published by the Division of Solid Waste Services in Montgomery County, Maryland. The U.S. government also uses Twitter, a microblog, to keep its citizens informed about issues as varied as health concerns, travel alerts, and rocket science. A **microblog** is an extremely short blog posting. For example, Twitter **tweets** are limited to 140 characters. Twitter postings often include links to full-length articles or blogs containing detailed information about a subject. When you subscribe to a microblog like Twitter, you receive updates in real time, as they're posted by the blogger. Given the restricted length of Twitter tweets, you can easily post or read Twitter entries from your mobile device.

> **QUICK TIP**
> Before you decide to follow a blog or a microblog, make sure that you are truly interested in receiving updates—possibly daily. Media overload might keep you from getting your own work done.

- **Podcasts**

    Governments also use podcasts to convey information. A **podcast** is an audio or video file meant to be played on an iPod or other multi-media device, such as a computer or handheld device like a Blackberry. Figure C-2 shows the Web page for subscribing to the Prime Minister of Canada podcasts, distributed by the Commonwealth of Canada.

> **QUICK TIP**
> The word "podcast" is a contraction of the words "iPod" and "broadcast."

- **RSS Feeds**

    Many governments also use RSS feeds to provide up-to-date information. RSS stands for really simple syndication. An **RSS feed** provides a subscriber with information from frequently updated Web content, such as podcasts, blogs, and microblogs. The benefit of RSS feeds is that you don't have to constantly check whether a site has been updated. When an update occurs, you are notified immediately. Figure C-2 shows the subscription page for podcasts by the Canadian Prime Minister.

- **Social Networks and Virtual Worlds**

    Governments use social networks so that employees can communicate and connect with each other within and across agencies. For example, the Environmental Protection Agency (EPA) has a group on Facebook that anyone with an EPA email address can join. Governments also use networks like Facebook and LinkedIn to post job descriptions and recruit employees. An exciting example of the government's use of a **virtual world** is NASA's CoLab, which uses the free software Second Life to let citizens and NASA scientists to meet in a virtual space to discuss data and ideas, and ideally, to create innovations in space technology. See Figure C-3.

> **QUICK TIP**
> Social networking is not the ideal tool for every workplace. Agencies and companies whose employees require high-level security clearances are often barred from using social networking—or even cell phones—in the workplace.

- **Wikis**

    Government agencies with similar goals have found that wikis are a useful tool for collaborating and sharing information. Intellipedia is one forum that intelligence agencies like the CIA and the FBI use to share information and plan operations. Although wikis can be posted on the Web, they can also be used behind the firewalls of any agency that needs to protect information.

Collaborating and Sharing Information

FIGURE C-1: Blogging by federal and local governments

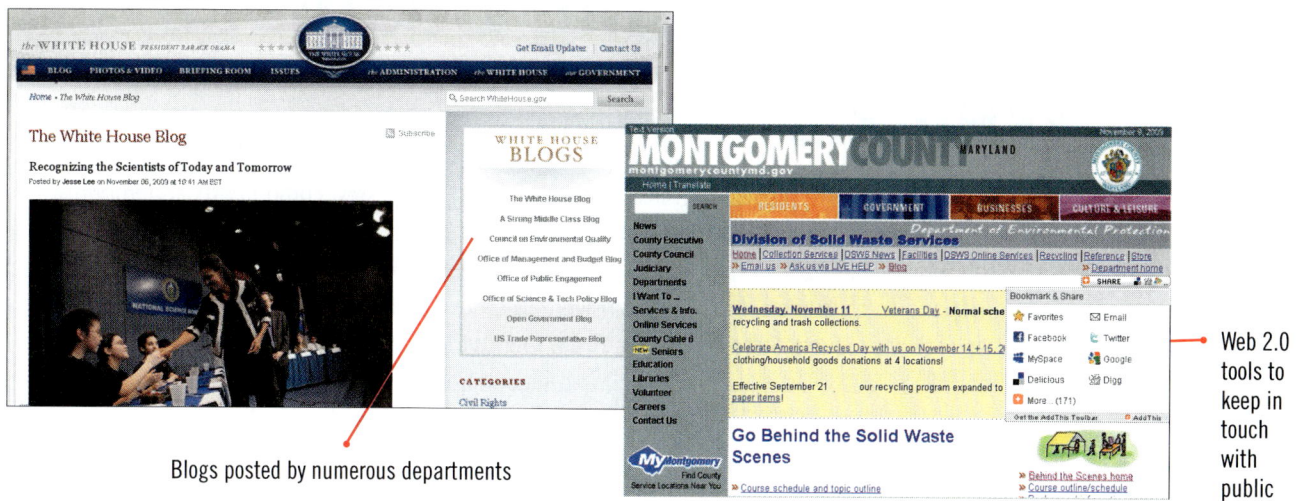

Blogs posted by numerous departments

Web 2.0 tools to keep in touch with public

FIGURE C-2: Canadian Prime Minister podcast page

Click to subscribe to podcasts and video

Follow the government on social networks

FIGURE C-3: Interacting in NASA's CoLab Island, a virtual world

Explore the surface of Mars on your own

Or meet with a fellow adventurer from halfway around the world and discuss your theories

Collaborating and Sharing Information

UNIT C Web 2.0

Understanding Business and Web 2.0

Web 2.0 technologies have provided invaluable tools to many businesses, cutting costs and improving customer support and innovation. Amazon is an example of an online business that jumped on the Web 2.0 bandwagon early on, and grew exponentially as a result. Other businesses use company-based blogs to educate and respond to consumers, live chat to answer customer questions in real time, and social networking sites to market their products. Still others create virtual worlds for their customers so that they can interact with each other online. Tactics like these improve brand recognition and encourage brand loyalty. Your group is interested in seeing how businesses have used the Web to succeed, and what effect the Web has had on a typical business model.

DETAILS

In order to use the Web effectively, businesses must recognize the following:

- **First impressions count**

  Because the Web is all about choices, first impressions count. A business Web site should captivate the customer and draw him or her in. It should showcase the brand in the most positive light possible, because a **brand** is not only the product or service you're selling, but the experiences the customer associates with it. The Web site should include eye-catching graphics, but should also convey the message that you not only care about your customer's money, but about her opinion. See Figure C-4. Customer support should be easy to find. Getting customer feedback should be a priority, customer concerns should come first, and the customer should know it.

- **Customers want to see the latest technology**

  Amazon is successful in part because its Web site is in synch with the latest technology. Many businesses have been slow to implement Web 2.0 collaboration features, simply, presenting their Web sites as virtual storefronts instead. A business should know which features will appeal to its market, and it should use them. Figure C-5 compares an early FBI Web site in 1996 and a recent version.

- **Customers have power**

  Remember that with the interactive Web, anyone can say anything about a product—and not only by posting comments on a company's Web site. Customers can post both good and bad reviews on social networking sites like Yelp, which can have up to 25 million visitors in a month. To monitor what is being said about a company online, a business can use a search engine like Google. Businesses can also use Web sites like Backtype.com, a **conversational search engine** that sends updates whenever a person with standing in the industry or area of interest comments about a company or other topic online. See Figure C-6.

- **Good business is about survival of the quickest**

  If businesses spent all of their resources responding to every disgruntled customer, there would be little time for product development and real customer service. The most successful businesses respond quickly to complaints posted on their own Web sites because that makes happy customers; however, they pick and choose which problems to deal with when they're posted on external Web sites.

- **Free products and services attract paying customers**

  Many businesses offer free samples of their products by encouraging customers to fill out an online form. They might also use the Web to create chat rooms and virtual worlds where customers can meet to discuss their products and make suggestions. Given the popularity of the Web with teens and preteens, using the Web in this way can create lifelong customers. For example, covergirl.com uses Web 2.0 technology to let users upload a photo and then use a "mirror" to try on different shades of makeup. The catch: Users must first provide a name and email address. Many online software businesses offer free versions of their software to customers.

> **QUICK TIP**
> Any good business will know when enough is enough when it comes to interactivity. If a site solicits too many responses in too many different ways, interactivity will lose value for both the customer and the business.

> **QUICK TIP**
> Businesses use this information for customer profiling and **data mining**, the process of gathering consumer information and then analyzing it in order to target potential customers.

Collaborating and Sharing Information

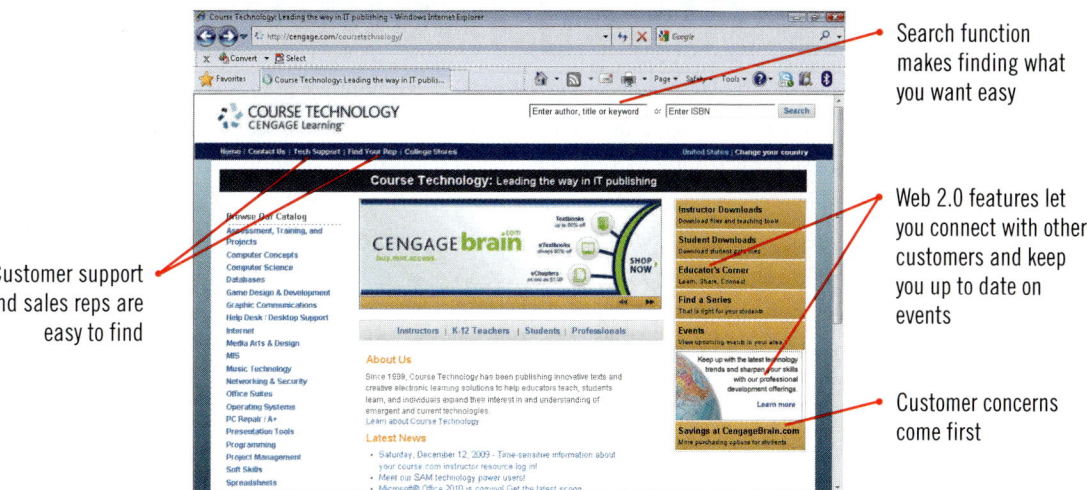

FIGURE C-4: Customer-centered features at Course Technology

- Search function makes finding what you want easy
- Customer support and sales reps are easy to find
- Web 2.0 features let you connect with other customers and keep you up to date on events
- Customer concerns come first

FIGURE C-5: The FBI then and now

- The 1996 version had simple links
- Current links include interactive Web 2.0 tools

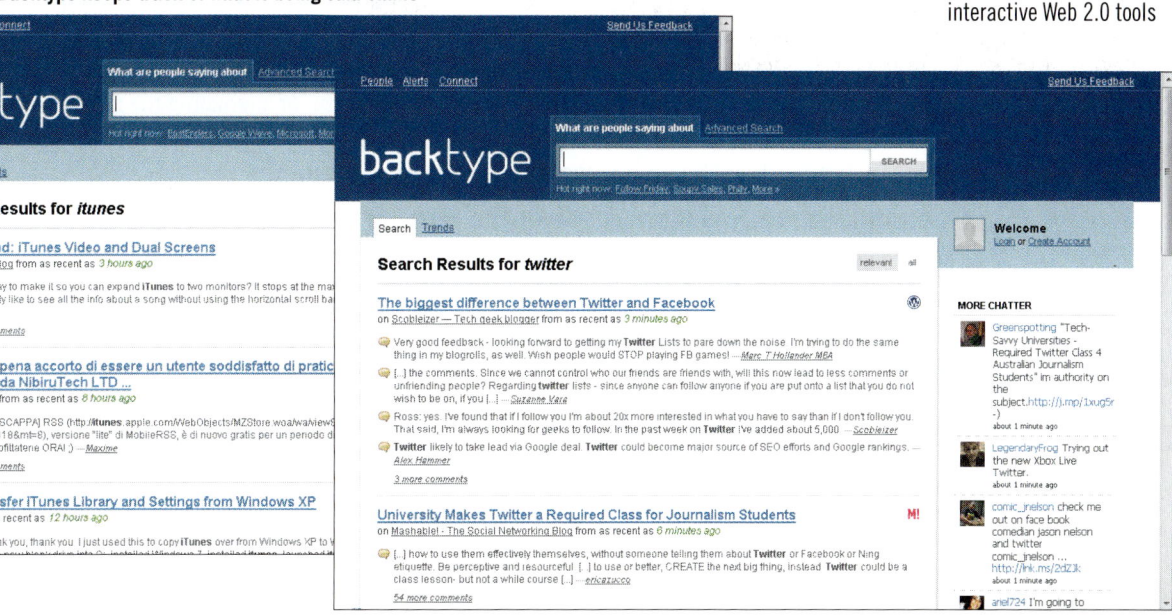

FIGURE C-6: Backtype keeps track of what is being said online

Collaborating and Sharing Information

UNIT C
Web 2.0

Scheduling Meetings

One of the biggest challenges in any collaboration is finding a time to meet. In the past, people had to phone back and forth or exchange multiple emails to find convenient meeting times. With features like the Meeting request in Microsoft Outlook, scheduling is less of a challenge, but in order for that feature to work well, meeting invitees have to share a mail server that has access to individual schedules. Web 2.0 scheduling tools let people from many different institutions find convenient times to meet without the back-and-forth of the past. Best of all, many of these tools are free. Your group has been texting back and forth unsuccessfully, trying to find a convenient time to meet about the project. You decide to take the initiative and use Web 2.0 technology to schedule a meeting time. You also take steps to get the group organized so that your collaboration runs smoothly.

DETAILS

QUICK TIP
You can also use Google Calendar (calendar.google.com) and share it with your group. If an event is modified, all members will automatically receive an email.

QUICK TIP
Once you find a space, don't forget to convey its location to group members.

QUICK TIP
Add time limits for the discussion of each agenda item to provide guidelines for how long each discussion should last.

You need to accomplish the following tasks when scheduling a meeting:

- **Find a convenient meeting time**
  One of the biggest challenges you'll face for any group project is getting everyone together. Professors sometimes allot class time to group projects, but more often than not, they will want you to get organized and motivated on your own. The easiest way to schedule a meeting is to use some sort of online software to do so. Figure C-7 shows doodle.com, a simple interactive tool. It requires four steps: Give the event a title and description, select possible dates for the event, specify possible times, and then send the event invitation to group members. As the organizer, you can send invitations yourself or use doodle.com to send the invitations. Invitees can go to the URL provided in your email and specify the times they can meet.

- **Confirm the location of the meeting**
  Imagine that you're all ready to meet at a particular time, but have no place to go. If you are in charge of scheduling the meeting, make sure that there is a room available for the time you plan to meet. Many schools have conference rooms that you can reserve online, or by signing up in a dorm or library.

- **Start a meeting with an agenda**
  An **agenda** is a list of items you plan to discuss at a meeting. See the sample in Figure C-8. Because groups can easily get off track, it's important to propose and agree on an agenda in advance of any meeting. In a meeting where everyone is essentially equal, as in a meeting of students working on a group project, it is a good idea for all participants to agree on an agenda ahead of time. One of the best ways to propose and revise an agenda is to use the collaborative tools discussed later in this unit.

- **Ensure that every meeting attendee understands his or her responsibilities**
  Meetings don't work if no one knows who's in charge of what. You might want to start your meeting by assigning a moderator to run it. If group members are resistant to having just one person take the lead, you might also consider setting some ground rules for the discussion, or alternating the moderator from meeting to meeting. As a rule, you should also designate someone to take notes, so that there is a record of what goes on at a meeting. Notes from a meeting are called **meeting minutes**.

- **Summarize the decisions made at the meeting**
  You might go into a meeting with very little information, but you should always leave a meeting with a list of assigned **action items**, or tasks individual members of your group have agreed to do. For example, if you are investigating how Web 2.0 technologies affect the way companies work and market themselves, have one person research online customer support, have another person research third-party blogs about companies, and have a third person investigate how different company Web sites draw the user in. When the group meets again, it can discuss and synthesize all of the information found by individual members.

Collaborating and Sharing Information

FIGURE C-7: Scheduling a meeting

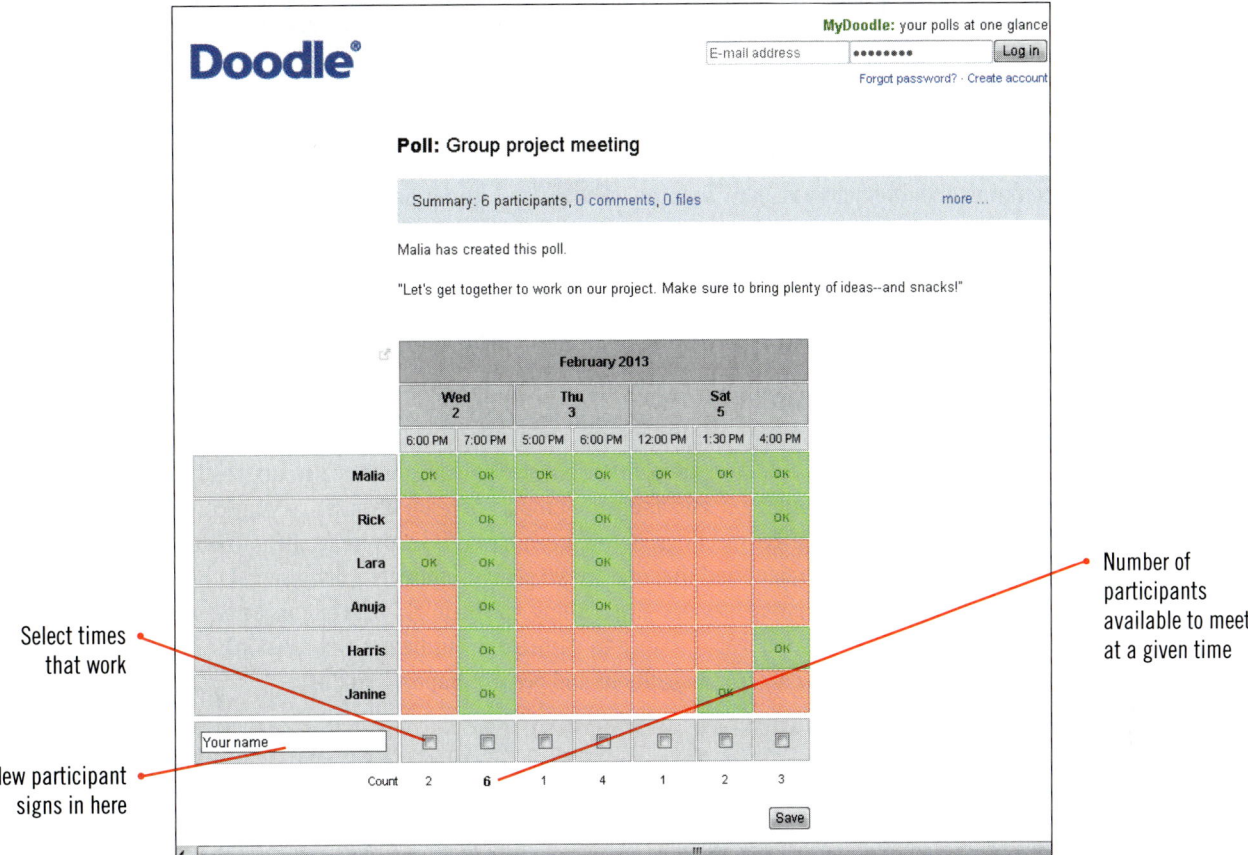

FIGURE C-8: Sample agenda

02/27 Development Project Meeting - Agenda

- Goals of Meeting
- Overview Development Project
    - LB has been hired to do initial development
    - We are reviewing the process and will supply the following:
        - Updated requirements
        - Milestones
- Process
    - How do we conduct reviews during development?
    - Will we track reviews online?
    - Set up flags for progress?
- Setting Milestones
    - What are our major milestones?
    - Get scheduling estimates from LB
- Action Items
    - TBD at meeting

Collaborating and Sharing Information

UNIT C
Web 2.0

Brainstorming Solutions

You've probably heard the expression "Let's put our heads together." Well, brainstorming on the Web lets a group put their virtual heads together to solve problems and innovate. When a group brainstorms, they articulate a problem or a question and then approach it from many different angles, all in pursuit of the common goal of finding the best solution.  Your group decides that the best way to come up with a futuristic product is to use tools on the Web to bounce ideas off of each other.

DETAILS

Some of the basic concepts about brainstorming include the following:

- **What are the advantages of brainstorming?**
  Sometimes hearing multiple perspectives on a particular problem will lead your group to a better solution than any individual would have thought of. When you brainstorm as a group, you bounce ideas off of each other. Ideally, brainstorming creates a superior product or result because everyone contributes. Brainstorming often occurs in face-to-face meetings, but that can have its disadvantages. For example, because of the way groups function, you might find that one or two people dominate a discussion. Others who don't feel comfortable speaking in a group may not say anything, so you might miss out on a great idea. With online brainstorming, everyone has an equal chance to participate. Furthermore, a "session" can take place over time, giving people time to mull over suggestions and perhaps improve on them.

> **QUICK TIP**
> You can also use bubbl.us for mind mapping ideas on your own.

- **How can you use software to brainstorm?**
  Similar to mind-mapping software, you can use brainstorming software in two ways. For visual learners, companies like bubbl.us let you create brainstorming sessions using graphics and words together, as shown in Figure C-9. For those who prefer a back-and-forth dialogue to describe their ideas, online discussion groups might work best. Figure C-10 shows a private online group set up in Facebook, and a brainstorm session set up at the BrainReactions.net Web site. Both companies provide a private, secure place to contribute ideas and reach consensus.

- **How do you moderate an online brainstorming session?**
  The best way to moderate an online brainstorming session is to set rules ahead of time. For example, you can ban negative or critical comments or phrases meant to shut down discussion. You should always promote a lot of ideas from each participant, no matter how off-topic they may seem at first. You might also consider setting a time limit and banning references not easily understood by everyone (for example, sports references and region-specific slang or jargon).

- **How do you narrow down the results of a brainstorming session?**
  Given the organic nature of a brainstorming session, if you keep the session moving along, it's very likely that the results will narrow themselves. You'll find that after considerable discussion, certain ideas take the forefront, while others are rejected by the majority. If you can't see this happening in the discussion itself, it's probably a good idea to put the ideas to a vote. Eventually, your group should come to a consensus on at least a few good ideas. The Web provides plenty of tools for online polling, as you'll see in the next lesson.

Collaborating and Sharing Information

FIGURE C-9: Sample brainstorm for visual learners at bubbl.us

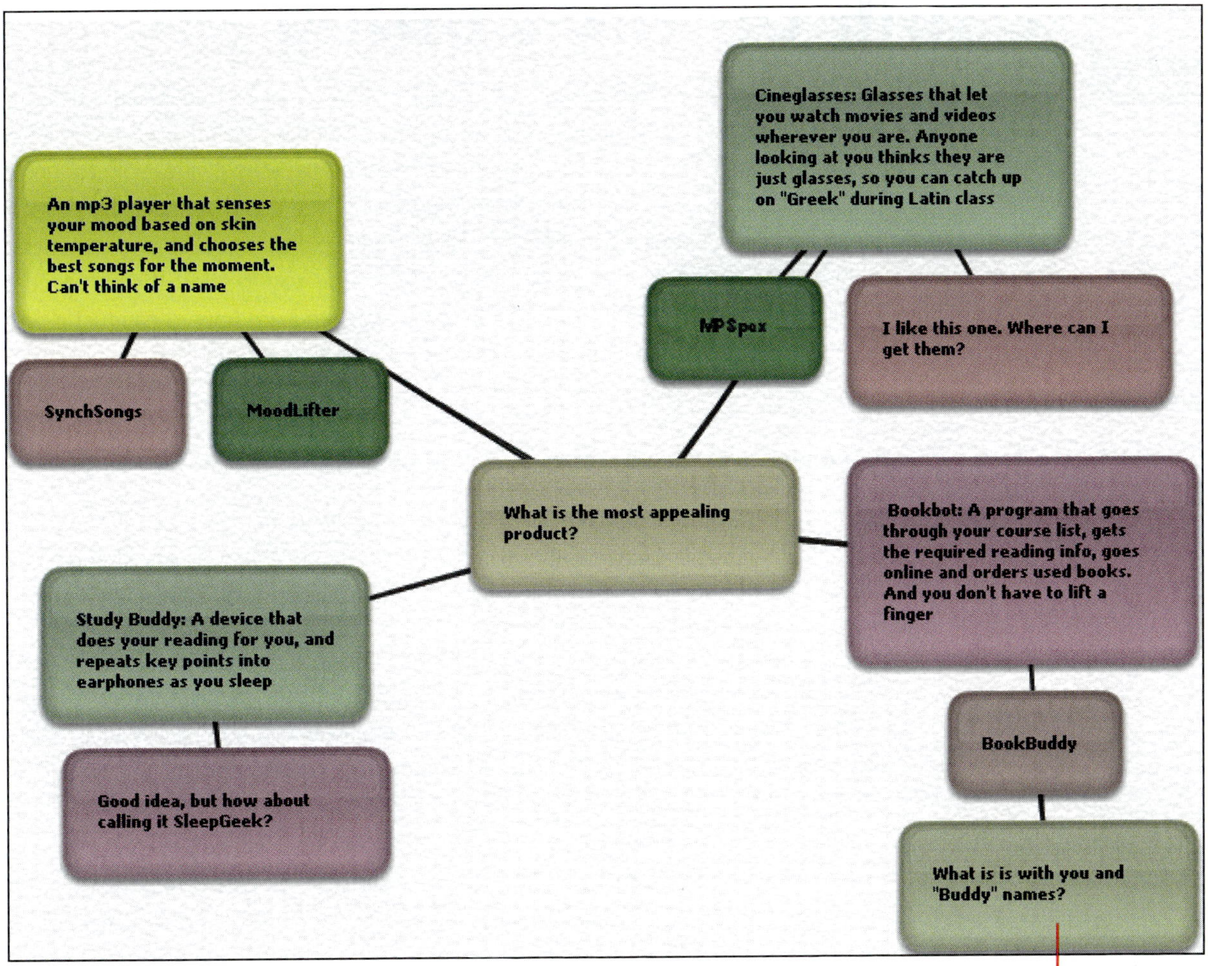

Avoid negative comments

FIGURE C-10: A private brainstorming group on Facebook and a brainstorm session on BrainReactions

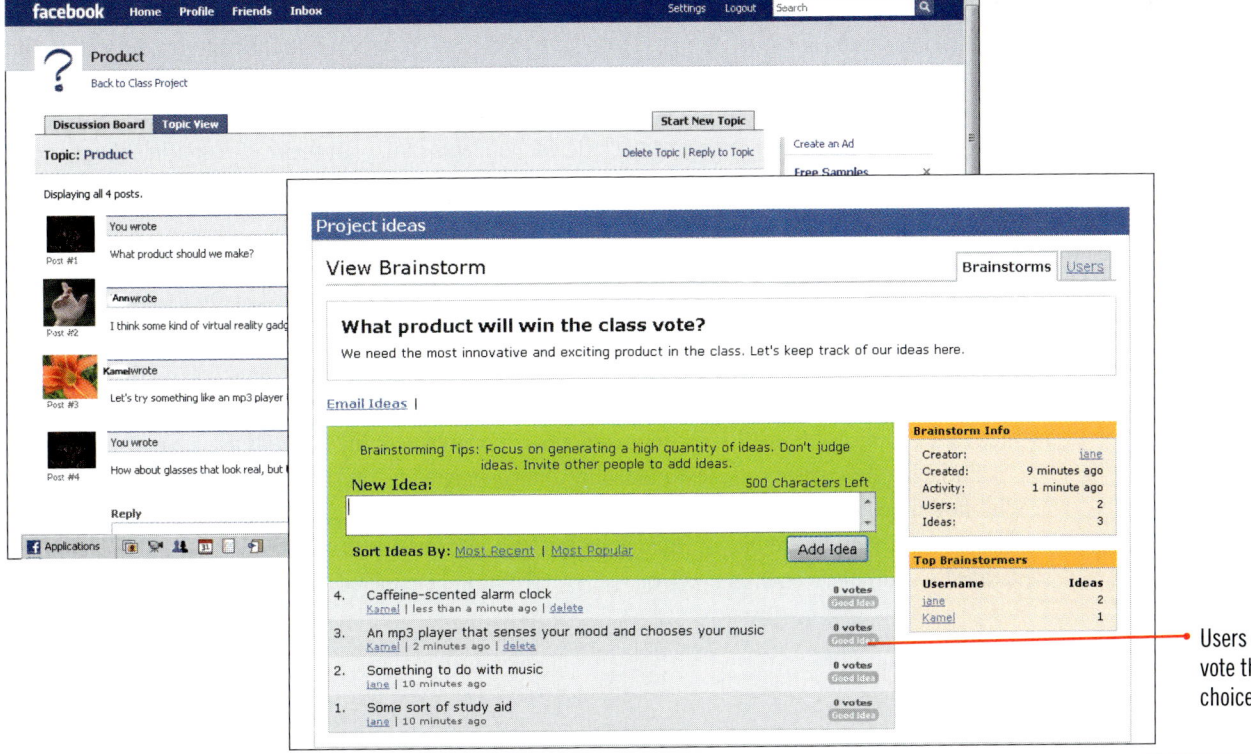

Users can vote their choice

Collaborating and Sharing Information 55

Web 2.0

UNIT C
Web 2.0

Using Online Polling

Politicians often rely on polls before making decisions or implementing policies; businesses use polls to learn about customers' likes and dislikes. You can use polls in your schoolwork as well. For example, if you are researching pandemics in your biology class, you might conduct a schoolwide poll to determine the percentage of students who plan to get the seasonal flu vaccine. You could conduct the poll the old-fashioned way, by sending people door-to-door on campus, or you could use the Web and text messaging to get answers more quickly. Your group has decided that one way to select the best product for your project is to poll the class on the brainstorming ideas. You want to learn how to conduct a poll, and also find out what software is available online.

DETAILS

When creating a telephone, face-to-face, or online poll, consider the following:

- **Are your polling questions objective?**
  One of the most difficult steps in creating a truly scientific poll is determining how to phrase questions without showing **bias**, or a preference for one answer over another. In practice, especially in political polls, this is rarely done, but if you want an accurate sample, it's best to make an attempt to be objective. In the flu vaccine example above, phrasing the question is easy: "Do you intend to get the flu vaccine this year?" With this question, you're eliciting a simple Yes, No, or Maybe answer. However, if you had instead posed the question as "In the 1970s, the last time there was a vaccination for swine flu, there was a controversy about whether or not the vaccine had caused the deaths of senior citizens. Do you plan to get the vaccine this year?" With the question phrased in this manner, it's possible your wording may have influenced respondents enough to change a Yes answer to No or Maybe.

> **QUICK TIP**
> Keep in mind that an online poll may not reach lower socioeconomic, non-computer-user, and geographically isolated groups.

- **Does your poll reflect a wide sampling of the population, or is it limited?**
  When you conduct a poll, make sure that your sample of respondents is random, and as broad as possible. If you are polling the student body, for example, don't poll only freshmen or only seniors, or exclude math or theatre majors. If you are doing telephone polling, don't only call people at home during the day, because then your sample will consist mainly of people who either don't work, don't work during the day, or work at home.

> **QUICK TIP**
> Poll Everywhere strives to allow only one vote per person—or more specifically, one vote per cell phone and one vote per computer. However, a person could conceivably vote once by cell phone, once by laptop, and once by desktop.

- **Does your poll allow people to vote more than once?**
  A poll should be democratic—that is, one person, one vote. If you have access to the college radio station and plan to run a poll by having people call in, remember that your results will be skewed toward 1) people who listen to your show, and 2) only those people who choose to call in. If you're familiar with *American Idol*, you know that voting by calling in is rarely democratic. Respondents can call in their votes multiple times, so the victor is often the person with the most persistent fan base, not the largest one.

- **Is your polling tool up to the task?**
  There are plenty of polling tools on the Web, and many of them are free, including polleverywhere.com, surveymonkey.com, and polldaddy.com. As with many Web tools, the free versions don't necessarily have all of the features you might want. It is a good idea to research any tool before you use it, and perhaps do a practice poll to see if you're happy with the way the tool works. One of the hottest polling tools on the Web today is polleverywhere.com, which has many of the features you would want for free, including multiple polling methods and a choice of formats for results. Figure C-11 shows two of the methods available for responding to a poll using polleveryhere.com: text messaging and clicking a link on the Web. Notice also that percentages in the top figure are updated as respondents vote. Figure C-12 shows a summary table, which is another format for displaying the results of your poll. You can also download your results as a **CSV (comma separated value)** file to open in Excel, or as a PowerPoint slide to include in a presentation.

Collaborating and Sharing Information

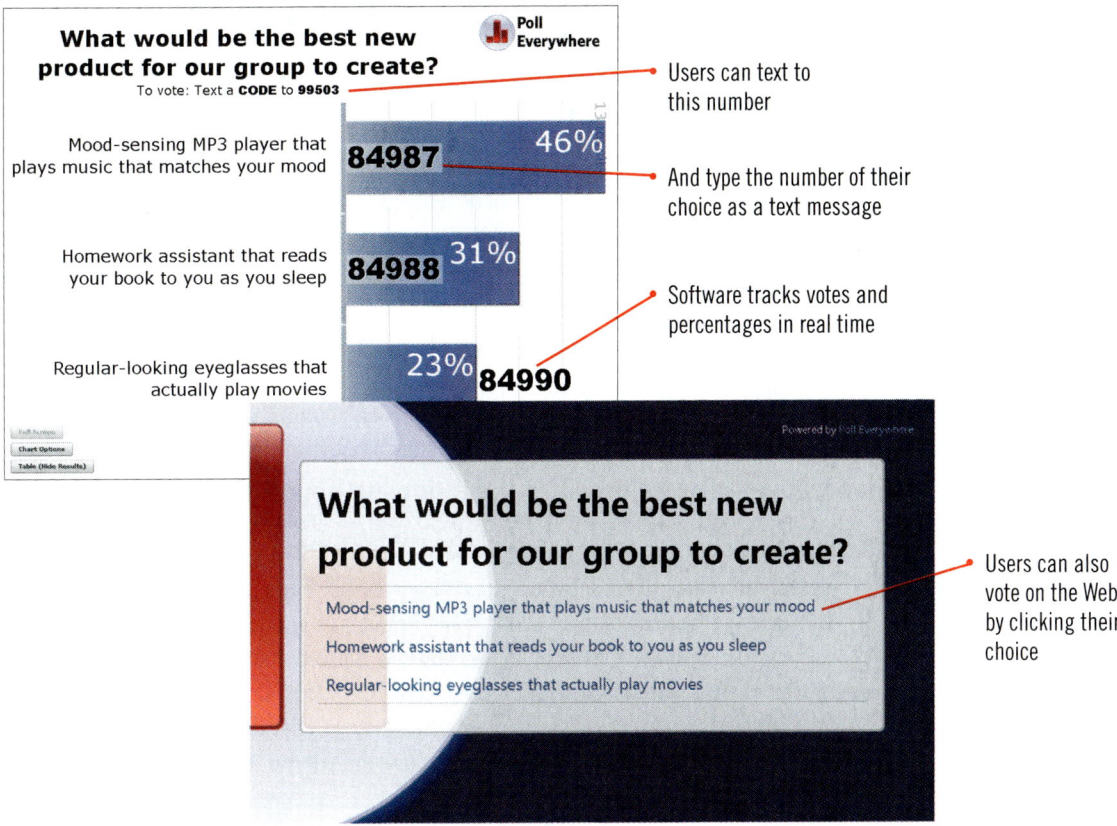

FIGURE C-11: Two polling methods at polleverywhere.com

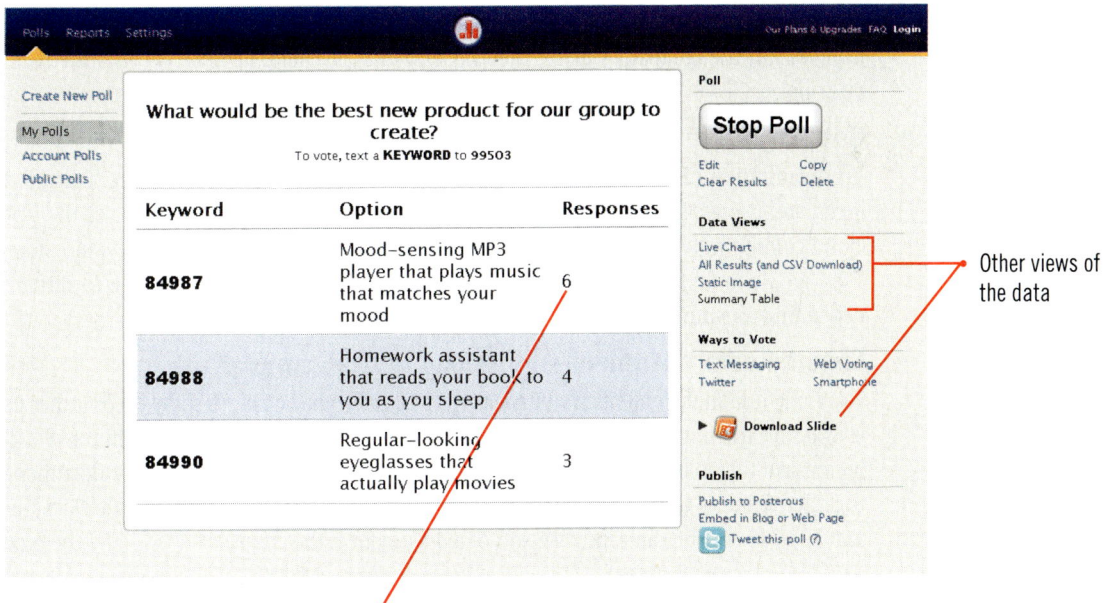

FIGURE C-12: Viewing polling summary in table format

Votes are tallied in an online table

Understanding push polls

Imagine that a pollster asks questions not to take the public's pulse on an issue or to compile data on which candidate is ahead in an election, but rather to push a respondent toward one idea or candidate and away from another. This kind of polling, which isn't really polling at all, is called a **push poll**. In the flu vaccine example, mentioning the swine flu controversy of the 1970s before posing a question about the current vaccine could be considered push polling, as the wording of the question might influence a respondent's "vote" by moving him or her away from getting a vaccine.

Collaborating and Sharing Information

UNIT C
Web 2.0

Using Collaborative Software

Collaborative software provides online document-editing and storage services to companies, governments, educational institutions, and individuals. These services give users the ability to access and edit documents from any computer, anywhere, and to collaborate with others on document revisions. The term for this kind of service, where software and user files are stored on a server on the Web rather than locally on a hard drive or company server, is known as **cloud computing**. Your group wants to explore the benefits and uses of collaborative software and determine if you can use it to improve the group's efficiency.

DETAILS

Collaborative software provides the following benefits:

- **Access to documents from anywhere at any time**

    When you use collaborative software like Zoho or Google Docs, your documents are stored on the provider's server, where you can access them at any time, from any computer with an Internet connection. You can also choose whether to share your documents. You can make them private, or you can give colleagues or classmates read or read/write access to them. See Figure C-13 for a sample list of documents on Google Docs and an email you can send to a collaborator when you share your documents. This kind of service is also called **Software as a Service**, or **SaaS**, because you use and pay for the software on demand, only as you need it.

- **Document and site security**

    Your documents should be as secure online as they are when they are stored on your laptop or desktop. In fact, sites like Zoho claim that your documents are actually more secure because of all of the different levels of security they provide. Even Zoho employees can't access your work, so you are guaranteed protection both from within the company's many firewalls and outside them. Figure C-14 lists the security measures taken by Zoho.

    > **QUICK TIP**
    > If the collaborative software you plan to use doesn't document an ironclad security policy on its Web site, think twice about using it. There are plenty of proven, reputable, and free options for you to choose from.

- **Cost savings**

    An organization can save money by not having to buy and upgrade software. Instead, IT departments can focus on business-specific activities, including development and deployment of their products, and let the cloud computing vendors keep them up to date with cutting-edge technology and storage solutions. While sites like Zoho and Google Docs offer free registration, you can also upgrade to different levels of services depending on your needs.

- **Simultaneous document editing and version control**

    You can work on documents simultaneously, and have your changes show up on other users' screens as soon as you save them. For corporations, this can mean thousands of dollars saved in travel expenses. For students, it can save valuable time and create true collaboration as they write and revise documents and presentations together, working toward the common goal of achieving their best work. Google Docs tracks changes by user, and lets you revert to an earlier version of a document if the change is rejected by the group.

    > **QUICK TIP**
    > The Google Wave (google.com/wave) collaboration tool lets you use text, photos, and videos to collaborate online in real time.

- **Flexibility**

    Online collaboration is an exciting new tool, but it isn't always one that's accessible. If, for example, you're on an airplane or on the beach without Internet connectivity, you won't be able to access your documents online. However, collaborative tools provide the flexibility of downloading the latest version of your work, updating it locally, and then uploading it when you once again have Internet access.

    > **TROUBLE**
    > Cloud computing does have its dark side, including the fact that it doesn't work well with low-speed connections, can be slow, and may have limited features.

Collaborating and Sharing Information

FIGURE C-13: Collaborating on Google Docs

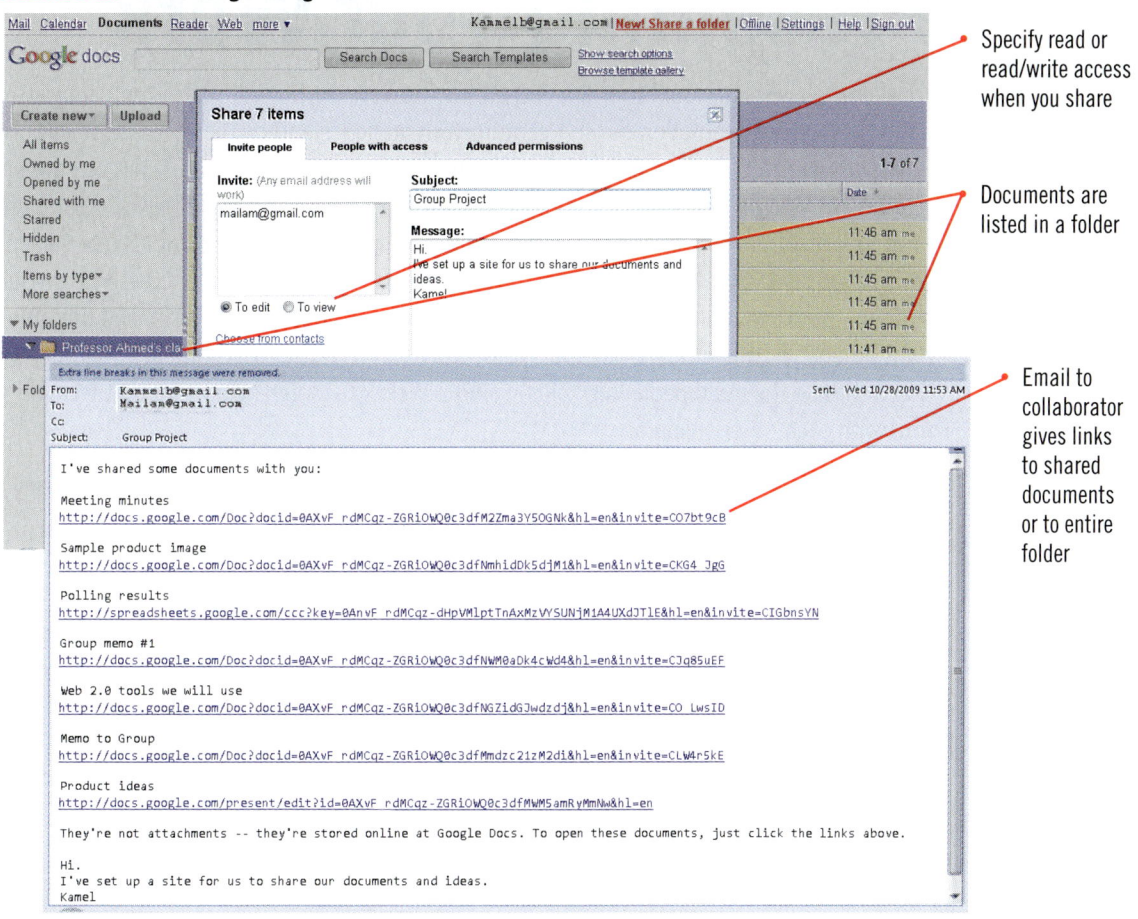

FIGURE C-14: Zoho security measures

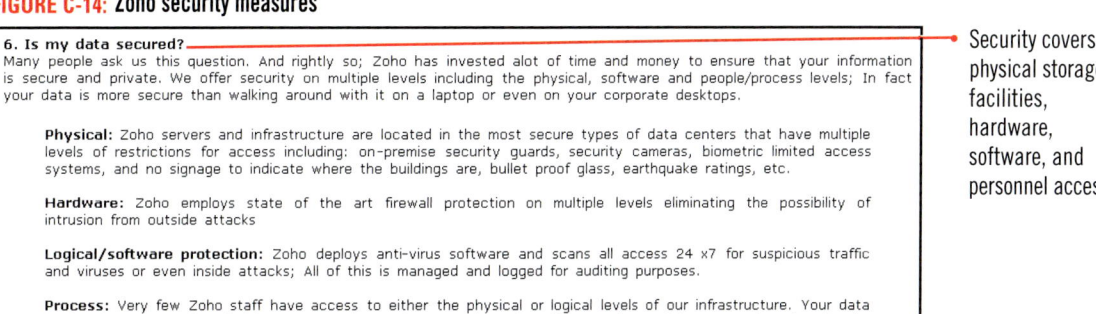

Doing business and governing from the clouds

Cloud computing is beginning to seem like a viable cost-cutting measure for many state and local governments. If they can outsource much of their information technology, they can save money, and when budgets are tight, that's an appealing proposition. In fact, the city council of Los Angeles voted to switch their entire employee email system to Google's cloud computing system. Businesses have also seen the appeal of cloud computing, especially since many paid services let them switch out the vendor's logo and URL and replace it with their own logo and a custom URL. In addition, sites like Amazon Simple Storage Service (Amazon S3) give developers tools to create custom applications that can "live" on the Amazon cloud. Customers pay only for what they use, and are charged per gigabyte of data storage and data transfer use.

Collaborating and Sharing Information

UNIT C
Web 2.0

Presenting Your Work

Your group has spent hours coordinating efforts. However, it doesn't matter how impressive your research has been if your presentation doesn't capture your audience and get across your main points. How do you go about getting organized for the big day? And once you are organized, what are the best tools for presenting? As you've seen, one of the biggest features of Web 2.0 is the ability to share information in real time. This feature is convenient as you work with colleagues on projects, but it's also valuable when you are ready to present your work.  Your group is making the final plans for presenting your futuristic product, an mp3 player that senses your moods and plays the appropriate music. The presentation has just the right amount of graphics, music, and video. Now you're ready to assign each member a set of tasks and then rehearse the multimedia sales pitch using a Web 2.0 conferencing tool that lets you share your desktops with each other online.

DETAILS

Preparing to present as a group requires the following steps:

- **Defining individual roles for group members**

    By now, your group has a personality of its own. Different people have taken on different roles. A successful group recognizes and takes advantage of the strengths of individual members. For example, one member might be the best candidate to moderate the actual presentation, another might be the go-to person for any technical questions, and a third might be in charge of creating or finding the images, music, or sound you want to include.

- **Rehearsing**

    Professors will often set time limits for presentations. This means it's a good idea to rehearse ahead of time so that you don't get marked down for going over the time limit or for being too brief. Rehearsing is also a good idea because it gives group members a chance to make sure they're all in agreement about who's doing what, and ensures that everyone is prepared so that there are no surprises on the due date. Rehearsing in front of friends or colleagues helps to reveal questions or weak points you might not have anticipated otherwise.

- **Setting up the right equipment**

    If your classroom isn't equipped with an electronic whiteboard, SmartBoard, or large monitor that can be attached to your laptop, you'll need to make sure you have the right equipment for making your presentation. If students in your class bring their laptops and if the room has wireless access, your problem is solved. You can use a Web 2.0 online conferencing tool to share your desktop with the people in your class—or even share it with remote users.

QUICK TIP
For a comprehensive list of collaborative tools on mindmeister.com, created by Robin Good, go to www.mindmeister.com/12213323#. Use it as a starting point, but do your research using Table C-1.

- **Choosing an online collaborative tool**

    There are countless online collaboration or conferencing tools on the Web. It's your job to find the best one for your particular needs. Factors you should consider when choosing a tool are listed in Table C-1. Figure C-15 shows the sign-in screen for a WebEx meeting at Cengage Learning, the publisher of this book. The WebEx conferencing tool lets you share your desktop with others during a conference call. You can even pass control of a desktop from person to person so that they can each handle a different part of the agenda or presentation. For example, if your team is giving a presentation on a new product, one person can present the overview, another the **specifications**, or product requirements, another the budget and profit projections, and a fourth can show the product in action—perhaps by using video and music.

Collaborating and Sharing Information

FIGURE C-15: WebEx sign-in screen

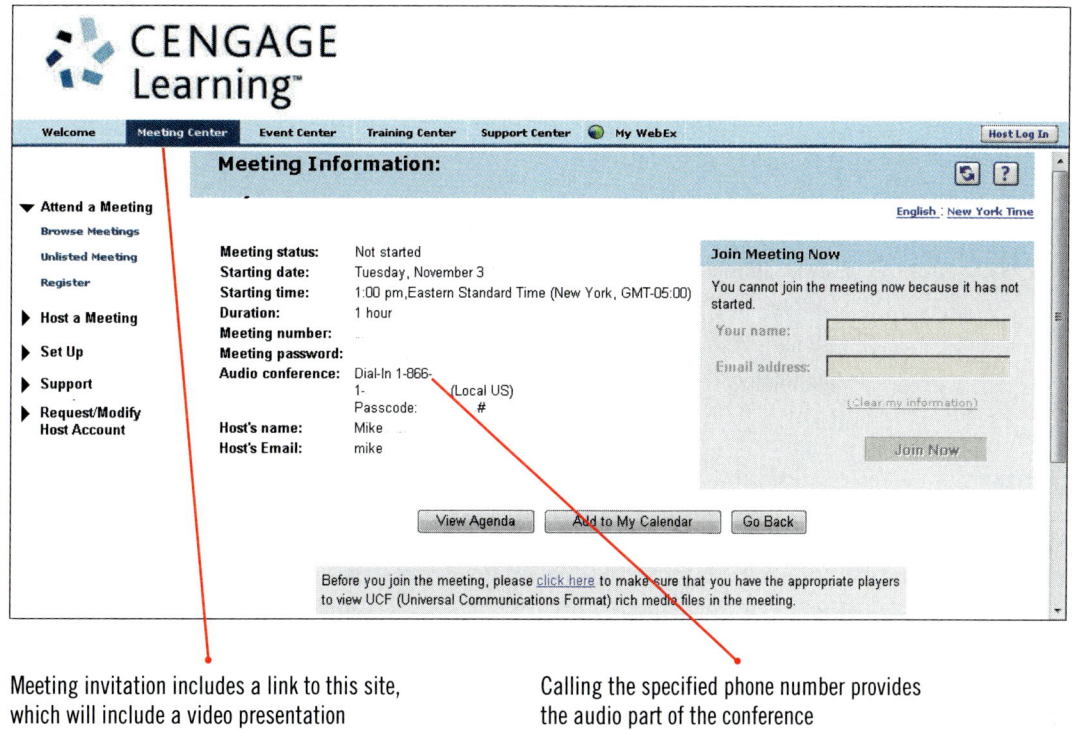

Meeting invitation includes a link to this site, which will include a video presentation

Calling the specified phone number provides the audio part of the conference

TABLE C-1: Factors to consider when choosing an online collaboration tool

factors to consider	details
cost	Some of the best online conferencing tools are free to individuals, small groups, and educational institutions.
desktop-sharing	If you plan to share your desktop or pass control to another user, you should ensure that the tool you choose has this feature.
audio	Unless you are simply collaborating on documents, you will want to have audio during your conference. Some tools provide call-in numbers; others, like Skype, make it easy for users with microphones to participate.
video	Video access goes beyond simple desktop sharing and lets you actually see the people in the "room" with you. Video participants need to have **Web cams** attached to their computers in order to be seen. Users without Web cams can see other participants, but cannot be seen themselves.
capacity	Many free tools have limits on the number of people who can participate in an online event. If you exceed that number, you will need to pay for services.
security	You need to be assured that any information you display or discuss is secure, and accessible only to meeting invitees.

Understanding presentation tools of the future

Tech-savvy audiences have grown weary of the slide-by-slide, bulleted-list presentations of the past. Accustomed to video games and special effects movies, your classmates, business colleagues, or potential customers are much more likely to respond to a presentation that uses similar features and effects. As a presenter, your challenge is to find the middle ground between static text and graphics and a dizzying array of special effects that buries your message. The Web provides many new presentation tools, and time will tell which ones capture the greatest number of users. Voicethread.com lets you combine music, voice, video, and text in your presentation. Participants can comment on a presentation five different ways and can even draw on it. Another tool, Prezi (prezi.com), lets you set up a presentation that looks a bit like a mind map. A Prezi presentation consists of a number of paths, which you can follow by using tools to zoom in and out, rotate, and pan to focus on various messages, drawings, and photographs. You can give your presentation on the Web, or download it and present it offline. You can also create content in Adobe Illustrator or Adobe Flash, and then upload it to prezi.com.

Practice

Key Terms

action items
agenda
bias
blog
brand

cloud computing
conversational search
    engine
CSV file
data mining

follower
meeting minutes
microblog
podcast
push poll

RSS feed
Software as a Service (SaaS)
specifications
tweet
virtual world

Unit Review

1. Name two of the major uses of Web 2.0 technologies by businesses.
2. Name two of the major uses of Web 2.0 technologies by governments.
3. What is the purpose of a blog?
4. Why would you subscribe to an RSS feed?
5. Why would a business use a conversational search engine?
6. How could offering a product or service for free make money in the long run?
7. Why is it a good idea to have an agenda for any meeting?
8. What might be the result of a polling question that shows the questioner's bias?
9. Name two situations that would indicate that your poll does not represent an effective sampling of opinion.
10. Name three benefits of collaborative software.

Fill in the best answer.

1. Twitter is an example of a(n) _____, a type of Web 2.0 technology.
2. An audio or video broadcast meant to be played on an iPod or other multimedia device is called a(n) _____.
3. Social networking is not usually allowed in government agencies that require a high level of _____ clearance.
4. If you want to see what is being said about your company or product on the Web, you might use a _____ search engine.
5. A list of items that you plan to discuss in a meeting is called a(n) _____.
6. Meetings are most successful when attendees leave with a list of _____ items.
7. When a group of people gets together either online or in a group and generates multiple ideas, it is called _____.
8. A polling question shows _____ if it is designed to elicit the response that the questioner wants.
9. A _____ poll is designed to have the effect of making the respondent have negative feelings about a subject or candidate rather than answer legitimate polling questions.
10. _____ computing is a Web 2.0 technology that lets users store documents online and pay for services as they use them.

Select the best answer from the list of choices.

1. **Which is an example of a microblog?**
   a. Facebook.
   b. Wikipedia.
   c. Twitter.
   d. Doodle.

2. **What does RSS stand for?**
   a. Regional syndicate status.
   b. Really simple syndication.
   c. Real-time reader synch.
   d. Rich site syndication.

3. **What is a virtual world?**
   a. An online site where users can meet as if they are physically in the same space.
   b. An online intelligence gathering site used by the CIA and FBI.
   c. An online security clearance level used by the government.
   d. Another name for a Web 2.0 browser.

4. **What is a conversational search engine?**
   a. A search engine that responds to voice commands.
   b. A site that finds audio files on topics you specify.
   c. A social networking site that connects couples with similar interests.
   d. A site that tracks online comments about products and businesses.

5. **What is the advantage of online brainstorming?**
   a. Multiple perspectives can generate better ideas.
   b. Participants can contribute equally.
   c. Face-to-face brainstorming sessions can get out of hand; online sessions are more easily moderated.
   d. All of the above.

6. **Which is an example of a good polling sample?**
   a. Respondents who are called between the hours of 9 a.m. and 5 p.m.
   b. All of the people in one neighborhood block.
   c. Friends and relatives.
   d. A random selection of people called at different times of the day.

7. **What is cloud computing?**
   a. A service that lets users create and store documents online.
   b. A meta-search engine that searches absolutely everywhere on the Web.
   c. A Web 2.0 meteorological tool.
   d. A cutting-edge computer hardware prototype designed for Web 2.0.

Independent Challenge 1

You are designing a Web site for your student government. In order to get ideas, you have decided to research how governments at the federal, state, and local levels use Web 2.0 technologies. Go to the Web site of a national government (not the United States or Canada) and explore it by clicking various links. If you can read more than one language, feel free to go to a non-English-speaking country. (*Note*: You can print or post this assignment. Please check with your instructor for assignment submission instructions.)

    a. Which Web 2.0 tools, if any, does the government use? Is it possible to subscribe to a blog or an RSS feed?
    b. Take a screen shot of the Web page that shows links to Web 2.0 tools or save the page as an HTML file.
    c. Go to the Web site of your hometown government.
    d. Which Web 2.0 tools does the local government use? Is it possible to subscribe to a blog or an RSS feed? (*Hint*: If your hometown does not use Web 2.0 functionality, find a municipality that does.)
    e. Take a screen shot of the Web page that shows links to Web 2.0 tools or save the page as an HTML file.

Independent Challenge 2

You are an intern for a new record label. In spite of its strong list of new artists, the company has been having trouble attracting customers. You have been asked to find ways to improve business and get the label name out on the Web. (*Note*: You can print or post this assignment. Please check with your instructor for assignment submission instructions.)

    a. Use the search engine of your choice to find and go to at least three record label Web sites.
    b. Using what you've learned about the success of Web 2.0 tools in attracting and keeping customers, choose the site that you feel uses these tools in the most effective manner.
    c. Open the word processor of your choice, and then answer the following questions:
- What is the most appealing feature of this site?
- Does the site use Web 2.0 tools and are the tools easy to find?
- Does the site use social networking?
- Is there a place for customer feedback?
- What features of this site would you use for your site, and why?

    d. Type **your name** at the top of the page, save the document as **Label20**, then exit your word processor.

Independent Challenge 3

Your political science professor wants you to create an online poll about an issue that's important to you. She suggests you research the different Web 2.0 online polling options available, choose one, and then poll at least ten of your friends, family members, and/or classmates using three questions related to the issue. (*Note*: You can print or post this assignment. Please check with your instructor for assignment submission instructions.)

   a. Use the search engine of your choice to explore at least three online polling Web sites.
   b. Open the word processor of your choice and write two or three sentences about the benefits and drawbacks of each of the sites you've explored.
   c. Choose one of the sites and set up your poll.
   d. Invite at least 10 participants to respond to your poll. Give respondents 24 hours to answer your questions.
   e. Using the tools on the Web site, save the results of your poll, then embed them in the word-processing document.
   f. Type **your name** at the top of the document, save the document as **MyPoll**, then exit your word processor.

Independent Challenge 4

You work as an intern for the chief financial officer of an environmental engineering company with clients all over the United States. The company consults with industries and advises them on ways to reduce carbon emissions and be greener. Although the employees have traveled a lot in the past, the company has recently decided to use Web 2.0 tools to do much of its up-front meeting with clients in order to reduce its own carbon footprint. It is also trying to cut costs. (*Note*: You can print or post this assignment. Please check with your instructor for assignment submission instructions.)

   a. Open the word processor of your choice, type **your name** at the top of the page, then save the document as **GreenCostCutting**.
   b. Use what you know about Web 2.0 collaboration to find information about the following types of tools: collaborative software, cloud computing options, and online presentation tools.
   c. Write a memo to the chief financial officer that starts with a paragraph about the benefits of online collaboration and document sharing.
   d. Add a paragraph that explains why you think cloud computing will work for this company.
   e. Give an example of an online presentation tool, include a screen shot of its interface, and list some of its benefits.
   f. Save and close the document, then exit the word processor.

Visual Workshop

Use the search engine of your choice to find the Web page pictured in Figure C-16. (*Hint*: Search using the title of the Web page, CCHS Learning Commons.) Keep in mind that the images on the site might change frequently, so your screen might look different.

   a. Which Web 2.0 tools does the educator use?
   b. Do you think these features increase the appeal of the Web site for students? Why or why not?
   c. Is it easy to use this site? Would you recommend this kind of site to other students?
   d. Could businesses learn from this site? Why or why not?

FIGURE C-16

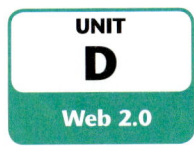

Perfecting Your Online Persona

Files You Will Need:
No files needed

You may not have thought of it this way, but if you spend any time online, there are actually two versions of who you are. One version, the one you most likely have pretty good control over, is the person who is reading this unit right now. Your actions, speech, and even your facial expression and body language, can influence how people in the room perceive and perhaps judge you. The other version is the one who lives online. That version is a bit more difficult to control. Nearly every action you take on the Internet creates a virtual profile that others can use to form their own opinion about you. They may use that profile to decide whether or not to give you a grant, accept you into college, or employ you.  Before she sends you out into the world to make use of your Web 2.0 knowledge, Professor Ahmed wants you to try to define your presence on the Web by controlling the things you can control, and avoiding the pitfalls caused by the things you can't control.

OBJECTIVES

Create your virtual self
Ensure privacy
Understand how the virtual world sees you
Understand professional networking
Choose professional organizations
Work with blogs and microblogs
Manage your e-portfolio

UNIT D
Web 2.0

Creating Your Virtual Self

Imagine that your studio art professor has asked you to paint your self-portrait. How do you think you would go about this task? Would you paint just your face, or your whole body? Would you paint for a particular audience? Would your painting be whimsical, comical, or serious? Which aspect of yourself would you want to express? Given this assignment, you would probably spend a great deal of time deciding exactly how you wanted to portray yourself. You should give the same consideration to the self-portrait you "paint" on the Web. Your Web presence, also called your **online persona**, your **e-persona**, or your **virtual self**, is what you look like online, and you need to ensure that the image isn't distorted. Professor Ahmed wants each member of your class to consider the elements that go into defining someone's e-persona, and explain the significance of each.

DETAILS

QUICK TIP
If you prefer to keep your email address, it's good practice to maintain one address for friends and relatives, and a second for professional communication.

QUICK TIP
Even your own page isn't airtight. If a friend likes a photo, he or she can download a copy and post it someplace you have no control over. You also have no control if you're tagged in a photo someone else posts.

The following elements make up your e-persona:

- **Your email address**
  Many people keep the same email address for years. Even if they change their **Internet service provider (ISP)**, they might still keep the **username**, which is the name that precedes the @ sign and domain name. A high school student who was cuteypie92 or DirtFan as an eight-year-old should probably consider changing that username when she starts applying to colleges or looking for a job. If you want potential colleges or employers to take you seriously, your email address is a good place to start.

- **Your profile photo**
  If you have set up your MySpace or Facebook account so that only friends can get to your wall or profile page, you might feel that you've done enough to control your online identity. However, remember that your profile photo is visible to anyone who searches for you. You might think that posting a photograph of you partying with friends or on the beach in your bathing suit is a good idea. It's not. If you want to post the kind of photo shown in Figure D-1, post it only where friends can see it, not on the wider Web for absolutely anyone to see. Even if you are very pleased with the photo right now, use your better judgment: In a few years, you might not want that particular version of you showing up in an unexpected place—like a prospective employer's desktop or inbox. That employer will, after all, be judging you based on your own judgment and the decisions you've made about your Web presence in the past.

- **Your social networks**
  Some people make a habit of collecting friends on social networking sites. Remember that the people you are linked to on these sites are, in turn, linked to other people, as shown in Figure D-2, and that all of these links are clickable, even if they don't take you beyond a person's info page. If you receive a friend request from someone you're not sure you know, ignore or reject it. If you do know someone, but don't know them well, think twice before accepting an invitation. When you have hundreds of friends, and allow all their friends access to your profile, you lose control of the distribution of your words or images.

- **Your tweets and blogs**
  On the Web, it's easy to type first, and think later. However, it should be clear to you by now that the Web has a long memory. If it were a person, you would probably say it was unforgiving. Not only is material that you post on Twitter or in a blog transmitted instantly all around the world, but once it's out there, there is no way for you to call it back. Therefore, as you cultivate and grow your online persona using Web 2.0 services like blogging and Twitter, try not to post anything that you haven't thought through very carefully. As a rule of thumb, don't post anything you wouldn't want a future employer (or your mother, for that matter) to read. You are leaving a personal data trail that anyone can—and will—follow.

Perfecting Your Online Persona

FIGURE D-1: You might not want a future employer to see this photo

FIGURE D-2: Your profile is linked to hundreds or thousands of others

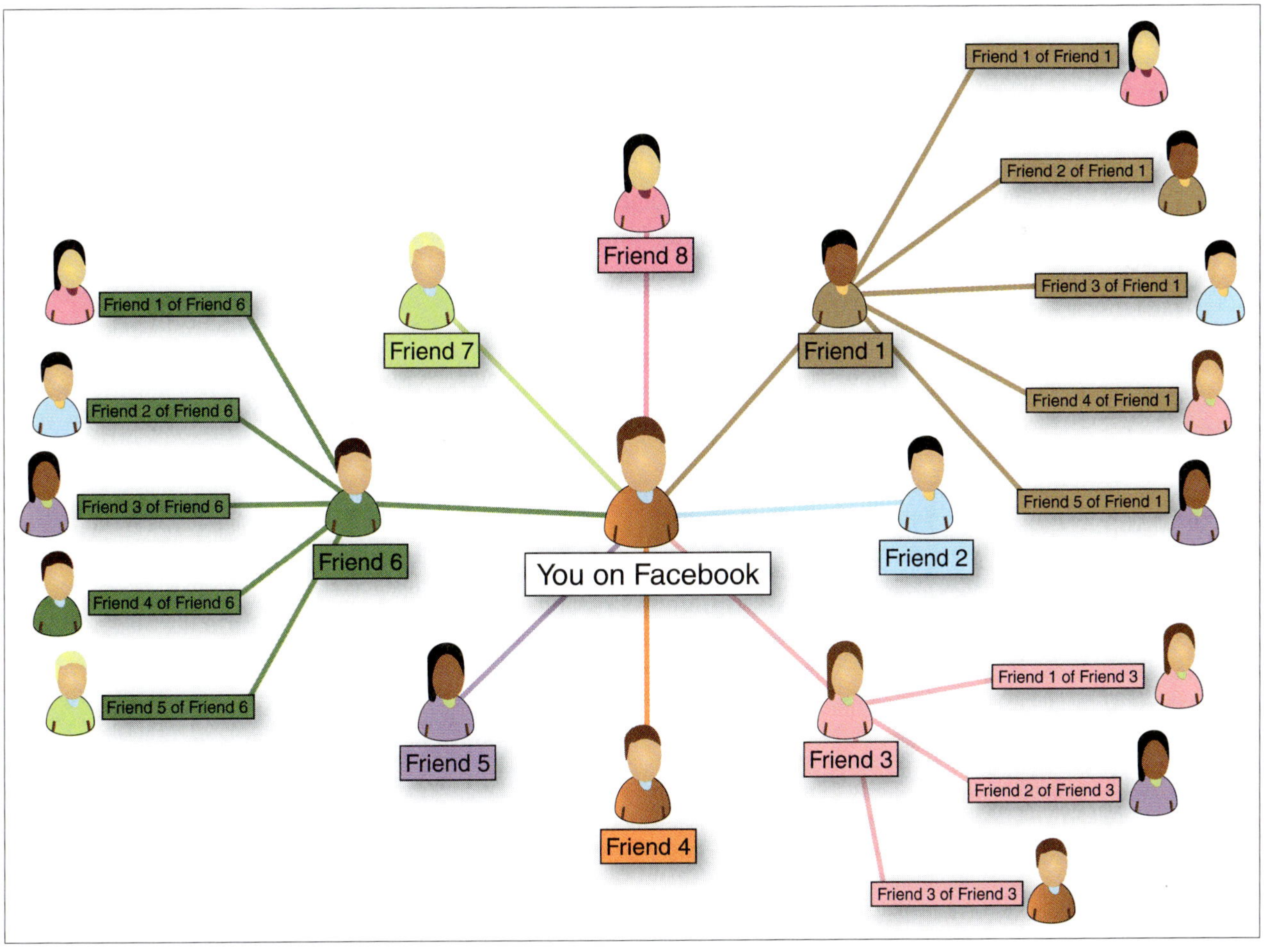

Perfecting Your Online Persona

UNIT D
Web 2.0

Ensuring Privacy

No matter how comfortable you feel with the security you've set up for your social networking account, there is probably even more you can do. You should be aware that there are measures you can take to determine who can search for you and what they can see, and to limit access to your personal information by Web applications. Professor Ahmed wants you to look at your own social networking accounts and see if you've taken the right measures to avoid sharing too much.

DETAILS

You should take the following steps to ensure that you maintain some privacy on the Web:

- **Control who can search for you and what they can see**

    Social networking sites usually let you control your **visibility** on the site, or whether other users can find you if they search for you. For example, Facebook, shown in Figure D-3, lets you set up your account either so that everyone who searches for you can find you, only friends can find you, or only friends and friends of friends can find you. You can also set up your account so that you have some control over what people see when they find you. For example, you can suppress your profile picture or keep people from contacting you or clicking a link to add you as a friend. You can also keep your list of friends private.

- **Control what information Web applications have access to**

    Many users of Facebook and MySpace use third-party Web applications to play games, send virtual gifts, and take or conduct surveys. When your friends run these applications, the applications have access to some of your profile information. You might want to change the level of access this kind of application has. Figure D-4 shows the options you have for controlling that access in Facebook.

- **Don't post information about your activities that is overly specific**

    Many people use social networking sites to post information about events, parties, and planned vacations. If you use social networking this way, make sure that you don't provide details that you don't want everyone to see. For example, if you post the exact dates that you will be away on vacation, there are no guarantees that someone won't plan a "visit" to your home while you're away. Furthermore, if you're planning an event, but don't plan to invite all of your friends, it would be wiser to send invitations by email or Web 2.0 sites like Evite.com or Doodle.

- **Don't post financial information on any site that is not secure**

    Don't provide any Web site with your Social Security number or financial information unless you are certain that the site is what it says it is. It's not difficult for a hacker to make a link look like a link to a reputable institution like your bank but have it take you to a phishing site designed solely to steal your identity.

> **QUICK TIP**
> Keep in mind that even if you set up your account so that only friends can find you, if you post something on someone else's wall, and someone who is looking for you happens to go there, your name and link will be visible to them. The same is true when you send an email message. It can be forwarded to people you don't know.

FIGURE D-3: Controlling your visibility on Facebook

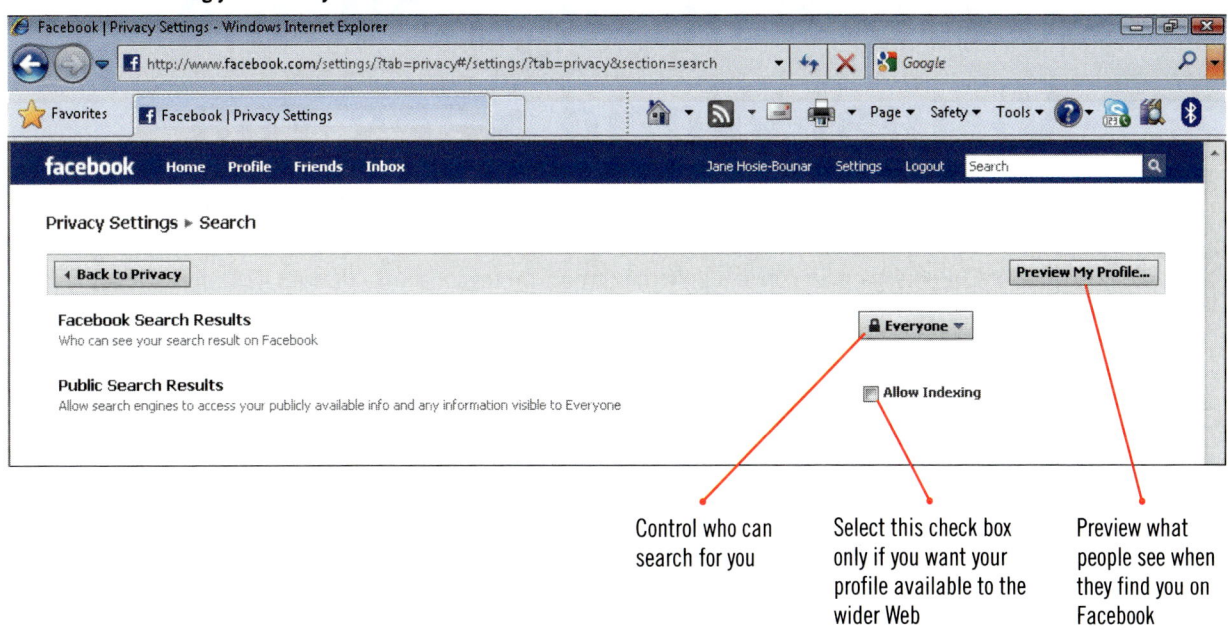

FIGURE D-4: Controlling application and Web site access

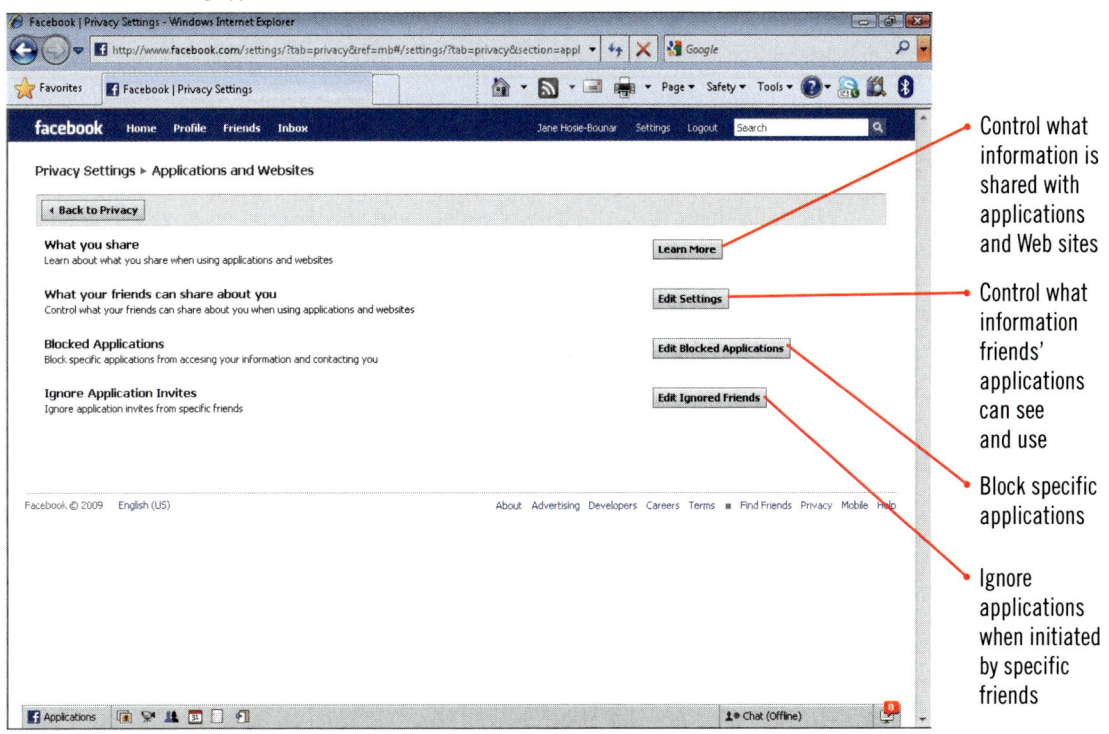

Perfecting Your Online Persona

UNIT D
Web 2.0

Understanding How the Virtual World Sees You

You have cleaned up some of the indiscriminate things you've posted on Facebook and MySpace. You've deleted immature or outdated blog entries. You've changed your email address to include your real name. Your online persona now conveys only the utmost professionalism—or does it? Unfortunately, if you have been indiscreet in the past—or even just a little immature, your cleanup work has only just begun. Fortunately, there are tools available to help you track down, understand, and, if possible, address the information available to anyone searching your online past. In Professor Ahmed's class, you are learning how employers use the Web to conduct background checks on job applicants. You decide to explore a few of the tools to see what you can find out about your own online persona.

DETAILS

When researching your online persona, ask yourself the following questions:

- **What tools are available?**

    Prospective employers can use a number of Web services to perform a **background check** to find out who you are, or at least who you appear to be on the Web. They can research the information you post on social and professional networking sites, your credit score, and whether you have a criminal record. Many of these services provide one level of information for free, and require payment for more in-depth details. Typically, this kind of service searches the **deep Web** to find data that traditional search engines might not find—for example, by searching the databases on social networking sites, public records on government sites, school records, or the billions of documents that reside on the Web. Sites like 123people.com and pipl.com, shown in Figure D-5, are two examples of this type of tool. Another service, spokeo.com, requires you to enter your Yahoo!, AOL, Gmail, or Hotmail email address. It then searches 48 social networks for information about you and your friends. A fee-based service, intelius.com, searches utility, court, and property records, among other things, and charges anywhere from about one dollar to $50, depending on the level of detail you request.

> **QUICK TIP**
> You can also set up a Google Alert by going to google.com/alerts and entering your name as the search item. Unless you are truly infamous, it's unlikely you'll get many hits, but it's worth a try.

- **How do the tools use information?**

    An individual doing research can use her judgment and decision-making skills to determine the plausibility of information she finds. However, Web tools don't discriminate. If something outrageous is posted about you—or someone with the same name—a background-checking tool will find it and report it. These tools appear to offer a "free" service, but they are free to use or sell the information you provide.

- **What is the best way to handle damage control?**

    Suppose you find something compromising when you research your online persona. What can you do about it? If you can locate the site where an unflattering photo or an untruth has been posted about you, you can contact the **Webmaster**, or person in charge of the site's contents, and request that the item be taken down. You can usually find the Webmaster by clicking the Contact Us or Contact link. Many sites also have a Report or Block feature that you can use to make a site aware of negative or inappropriate content. If you aren't successful in getting the posting removed, you can at least prepare yourself for possible questions about it. Individuals or companies can also hire a **reputation management firm** to help clean up negative posts and improve someone's online reputation. These services are typically fee-based.

> **QUICK TIP**
> You can also respond to negative posts about you with a post on your Facebook page or blog. However, doing so will bring the matter to the attention of people who may not have been aware of it otherwise.

- **What if someone is pretending to be me online?**

    When you research your online persona, you might find that an **imposter** has set up a social networking account and is pretending to be you. This situation can be extremely damaging to your reputation, and you should try to correct it immediately. Unfortunately, that is not always an easy thing to do. The burden is on you to prove that you are the person you say you are, and that your identity has been stolen. Sites like MySpace provide specific instructions for dealing with an imposter, as shown in Figure D-6. Other sites might require you to dig a bit to find the procedure for undoing the damage. No matter how difficult it is to take down an imposter account, you should invest the time it takes.

Perfecting Your Online Persona

FIGURE D-5: Searching for people on the deep Web

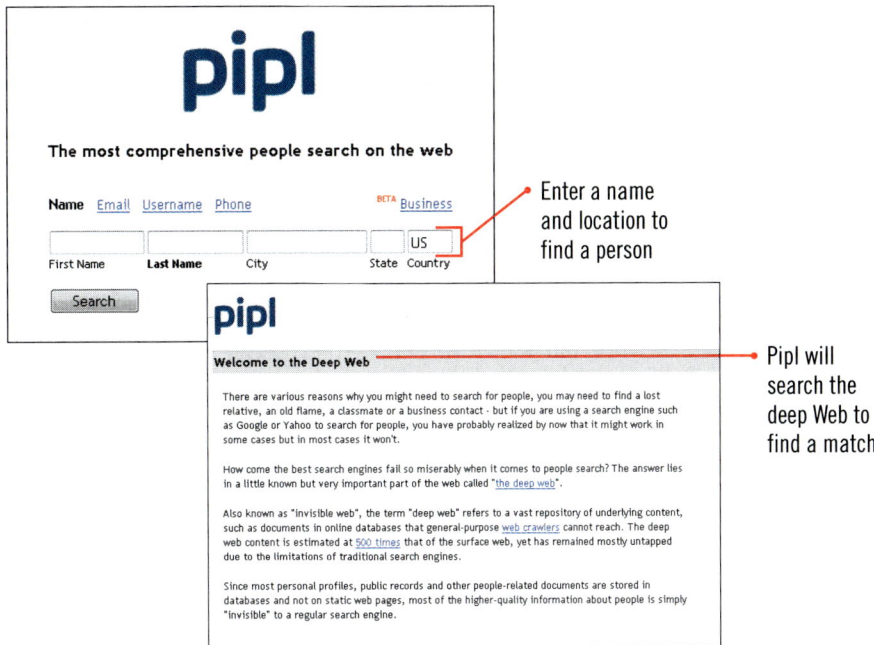

FIGURE D-6: Deleting an imposter profile on MySpace

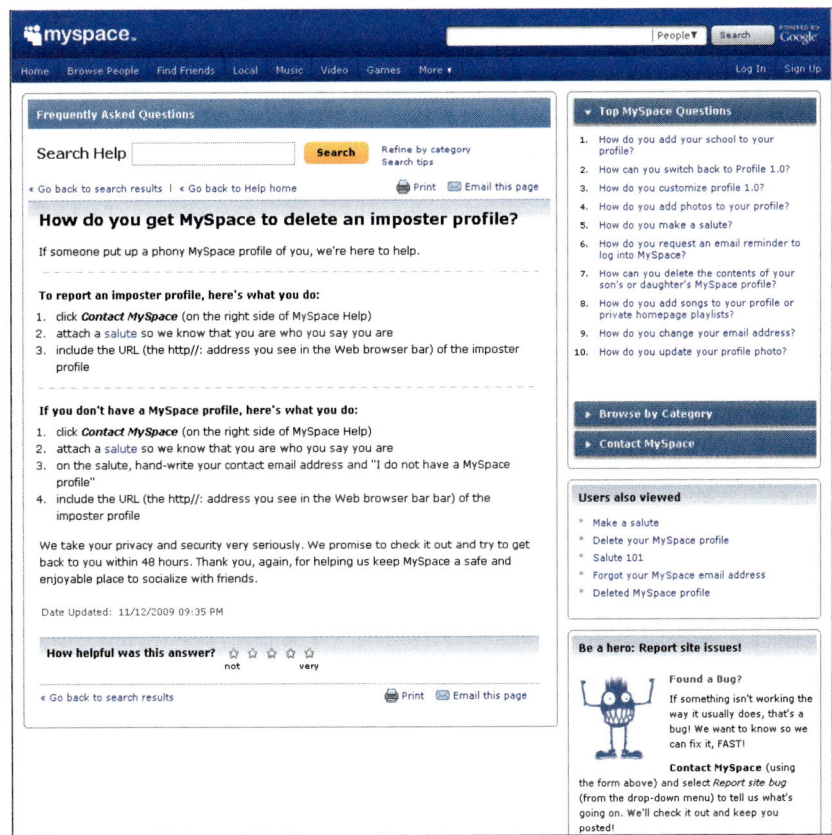

A warning about posting photos and videos

When it first became possible to post photographs and videos on the Web, the appeal was obvious. Families and friends separated by miles could instantly share pictures of newborn babies, weddings, graduations, and special events. However, even today, many people don't realize how difficult it is to remove media from the Web once it's there. Funny or offensive photos and videos go **viral**, traveling around the world in a matter of minutes via sites like YouTube, MySpace, and Facebook. Strangers take images out of context and leave inappropriate comments on Web sites. What started as a personal posting, meant to be shared among friends, might very well end up on the news or as fodder for a late-night comedian.

UNIT D
Web 2.0

Understanding Professional Networking

Even if you are still a student, it's never too early to start exploring the world of professional networking. A professional networking site connects people based on their shared professions, industries, contacts, and goals. A professional network can be local, like a chamber of commerce. It can also be global or industry-specific. Like a social networking site, a professional networking site connects you not only to the people in your immediate circle, but also to the people those people are connected to. You can use these connections to find work, collaborate on projects, share information, and find potential employees. As part of your study of Web 2.0 tools, Professor Ahmed wants you to explore the possibilities of professional networking and start thinking about how you would present yourself on a professional network.

DETAILS

When creating a professional profile, you should remember the following:

- **Choose the professional networking site that works best for you**

  Before you join a professional networking site, do some research. Use the search skills you've developed to find information about networking sites in the field you're interested in, and about general networking sites like LinkedIn. Ask professionals in your industry which sites they consider the most helpful. If a site requires an invitation, go through your list of colleagues and friends to see if there's anyone who might invite you.

- **Consider the cost**

  Some professional networks require a fee. Others, like LinkedIn, are free for basic services but require payment for more comprehensive services, as shown in Figure D-7. Before you pay for a service, make sure you have exhausted all of the features of the free service and that the paid service provides value for you. For example, a site like LinkedIn lets you search for a person, connect with a friend or colleague, forward someone's profile to a contact, and search for a job—all for free.

- **Use a "headline" that makes you stand out**

  Remember that first impressions count. Because the level of detail a person can see about you on many professional networking sites depends on that person's level of access, your main descriptor (called a **headline** on LinkedIn) should be specific and to the point. If you want to emphasize your experience in a particular position, consider using the word "experienced" in your descriptor. For example, "Experienced Project Manager" shows you in a different light than simply "Project Manager." See Figure D-8. However, don't give yourself a title you haven't earned.

- **Remember that your profile is serious business**

  When you create a profile on a professional networking site, you need to paint yourself in the most professional light possible. The language and organization of your profile should convey the fact that you are serious about your career. To create a successful profile, you should familiarize yourself with industry job titles, job descriptions, and vocabulary and use them to your benefit. Remember that companies searching a site like LinkedIn for a potential employee can view hundreds of results. Your profile should be specific enough to attract employers in your industry, but not so specific it eliminates you from consideration for jobs that aren't an exact match with your college major or past employment.

- **Don't exaggerate**

  It's true that you want to present yourself in the best light possible, but remember that you are not writing fiction: Be honest in your self-assessment. Don't exaggerate your experience or say you have a skill set you don't have. You are bound to be found out—if not online, then in the office soon after you start a job for which you are ill-prepared. Instead, show your enthusiasm by describing your career goals, and build up your image by linking to reputable colleagues and professors and asking them to recommend you.

> **QUICK TIP**
> LinkedIn also includes a "Grad Guide" at http://grads.linkedin.com, designed especially for college graduates preparing to enter the workforce. It provides training and advice for using LinkedIn services, and is an invaluable tool.

Perfecting Your Online Persona

FIGURE D-7: LinkedIn member service levels

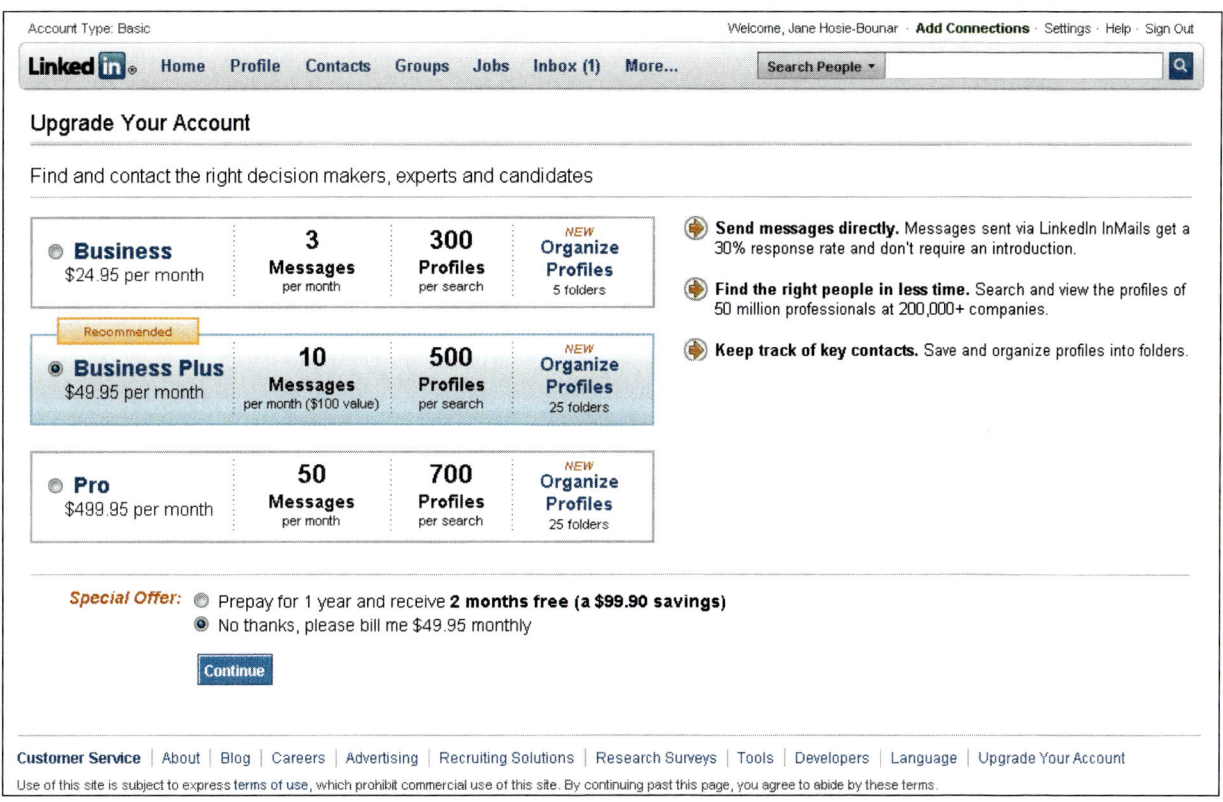

FIGURE D-8: Advice for creating a headline on LinkedIn

Perfecting Your Online Persona

Choosing Professional Organizations

Establishing contact with people who work in your chosen career is a great way to get ready for the "real world," or to make connections with people who can help you find an internship during your school years. In the past, you could enroll in a professional organization either online or through the mail, but in order to meet other members, you had to search for and then attend the local branch or chapter meetings for that organization. However, many professional organizations now include Web-based memberships that let people meet and network with each other online. They also provide other services that can prove invaluable to both a novice and a seasoned professional. Professor Ahmed wants you to explore the broad range of professional organizations online and see what services they offer.

DETAILS

Professional organizations may offer the following services:

- **Membership**

  Like many of the Web 2.0 tools and sites you've already explored, professional organizations often offer various membership levels. Student memberships are the most reasonably priced. Through membership, you can connect with **mentors**, or people who can help guide you as you develop the skills you'll need in your career. Membership in a professional organization is also part of your e-persona, and can help define who you are. Figure D-9 shows the student membership benefits of the International Association of Business Communicators (IABC).

- **Training and development**

  To see if an organization is right for you, try to find its **mission statement**, or its stated goals as an organization. Figure D-10 shows the mission statement of the International Association for Energy Economics (IAEE), an organization devoted to "professional communication and exchange" for people interested in energy economics. One of the most valuable resources a professional organization can provide is training. Many online professional organizations post information about seminars offered around the country or around the world. They also run **webinars**, which are seminars conducted online. The IABC, shown in Figure D-9, lets members access **teleseminars**, or recordings of earlier presentations about pertinent topics. In addition, many organizations can direct you to classes to help you get certified in your field.

- **White papers and other publications**

  Online professional organizations often include a wealth of resources, including **white papers**, which are informational, authoritative reports about topics of interest to organization members. You can also subscribe to online journals and find links to other sites related to your profession.

- **Networking**

  Online professional organizations also promote the flow of information between specialists. This kind of networking not only furthers careers, it also contributes to the general knowledge of a group, and can benefit not only its members, but the people those members deal with. For example, Sermo (sermo.com), shown in Figure D-11, is a resource that lets physicians share insights about the medical profession in general, and also lets them collaborate to work through difficult cases.

- **Job postings**

  Many online sites let members post and search for jobs. Because a professional organization is specifically devoted to a particular field, its job resources can be even more valuable to you than the resources found at a more general professional networking site like LinkedIn.

Perfecting Your Online Persona

FIGURE D-9: Student membership benefits of the IABC

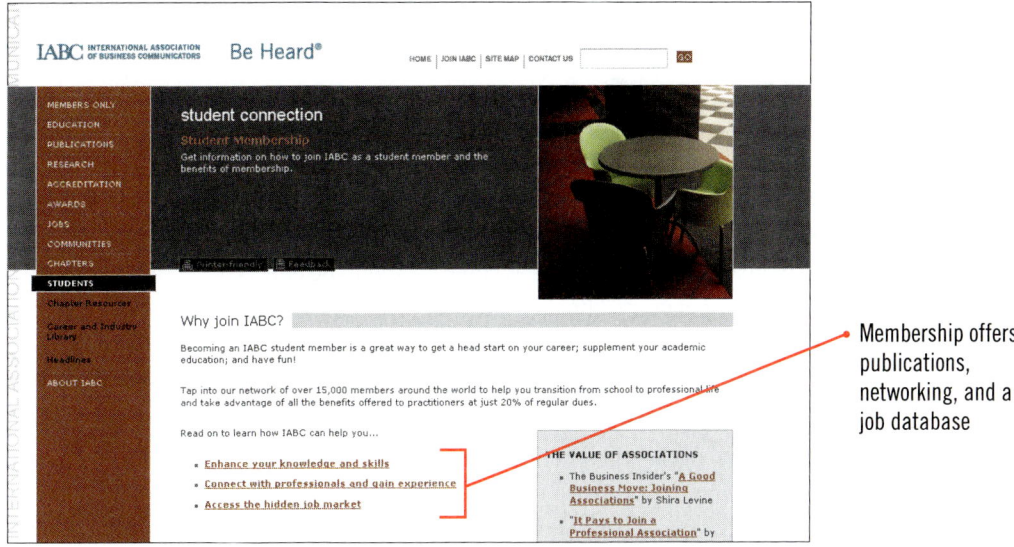

FIGURE D-10: Mission statement of the IAEE

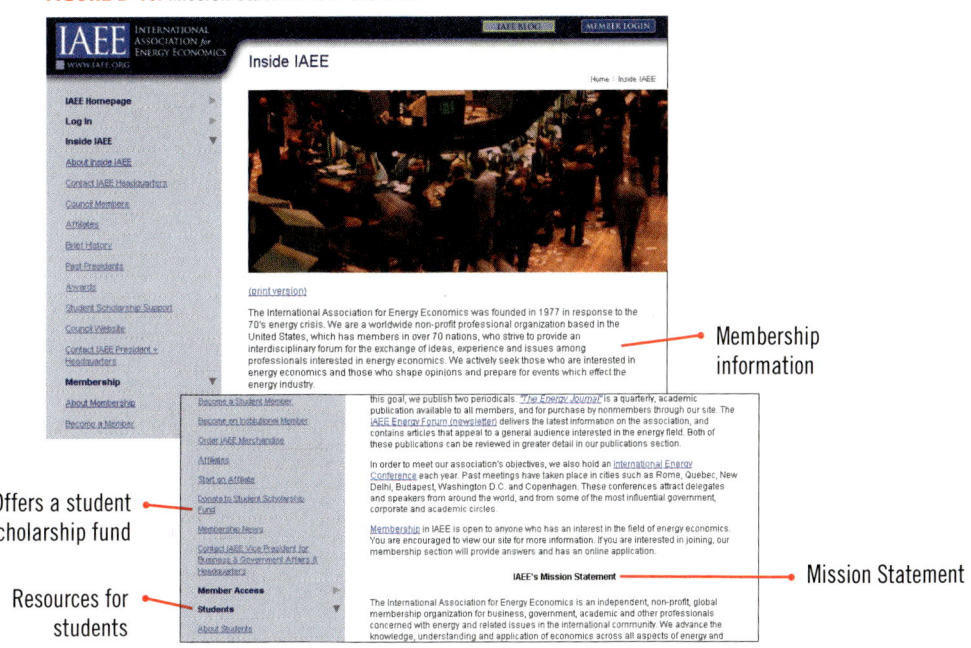

FIGURE D-11: A networking resource for physicians

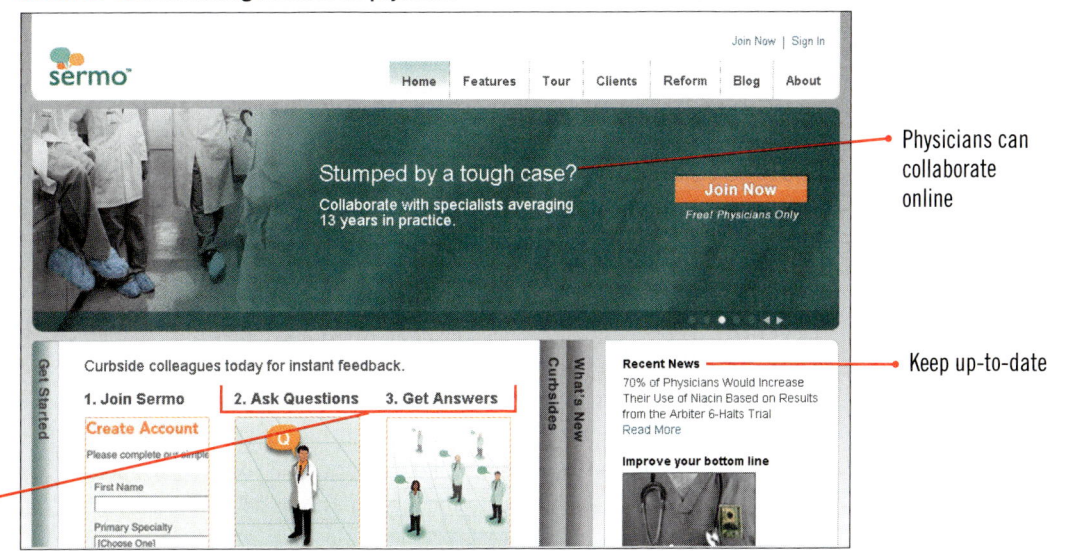

Perfecting Your Online Persona

UNIT D
Web 2.0

Working with Blogs and Microblogs

When you write a blog or develop a following on a microblog site like Twitter, you are adding more brushstrokes to your e-persona. You should take the same care in composing blog entries that you would take when writing a résumé, because as you have seen, the effects of your online actions have no expiration date. This does not mean you shouldn't join the world of bloggers. If you have something to say, and can say it well, you should consider starting a blog. Maintaining a blog can convey your seriousness to college admissions officers, potential employers, and business partners. It can provide a different perspective on who you are—and it is a perspective you have a great deal of control over. Professor Ahmed wants you to research a few of the more popular blogging sites and decide how you would approach the task of writing your own blog.

DETAILS

You should ask yourself the following questions before starting a blog:

- **What is the focus of my blog?**
  A blog can have any focus you want it to have. For example, your blog can educate your readership on a particular subject. A **corporate blogger** might present weekly updates on the latest products or technology offered by a company. A blog can have an editorial focus with the intent of persuading readers to adopt a particular point of view. A blog can also be entertaining—for example, a blogger might simply review and recommend books, movies, or music. If you want to get a good sense of the types of blogs on the Web, visit technorati.com. Technorati has posted an extensive directory of blogs categorized by subject, as shown in Figure D-12.

- **How do I find readers for my blog?**
  As a blogger, you can write independently or you can blog as part of an organization. You should be aware that it takes time for a blog to build momentum and find readers. One way to develop a readership is to post a link to your blog on your social networking site, send the link as a text message to all of your contacts, or include a link as part of your email signature. If your blog is meant for colleagues or fellow students, you can also post blog links on any professional or student networks to which you belong.

- **Should I post a microblog?**
  Because microblogs only allow a limited number of characters, you need to be good at distilling an idea down to its most important expression. A microblog, by nature, can only present a full picture of you if your posts are frequent and focused—and if a reader has the patience to go through multiple posts. The most significant use of microblogs has been during natural disasters and political upheavals. For example, during the election crisis in Iran in 2009, Iranian citizens kept the world informed through frequent microblog postings that included text, audio, and video. Through microblogs, information was spread even more quickly than it was in mass media like television and radio.

- **What blogging tools are available?**
  With the research skills you've developed in this course, you can easily find a blogging tool that suits your needs. Two of the more popular tools can be found at blogger.com (a Google site) and wordpress.com, shown in Figure D-13. Many sites automate the process of creating a blog, taking you step by step through a wizard. All you have to do is provide a title and the content.

- **What are the features of a successful blog?**
  As with other Web 2.0 applications, the most successful blogs are visually pleasing, user-friendly, and easy to navigate. They combine text with photographs, video, and links to related sites. They are well organized and archived in a way that makes it easy to find old posts. They develop an audience because they have a strong voice, and because they are up-to-date and relevant. If you do plan to start a blog, make sure that you're willing to make a long-term commitment.

> **QUICK TIP**
> If you want to have fun with a blog but remain anonymous, you can invent an alter ego by blogging under a different name. However, remember that if your blog becomes popular, it's possible someone will find out your true identity.

Perfecting Your Online Persona

FIGURE D-12: Technorati lists blogs by category

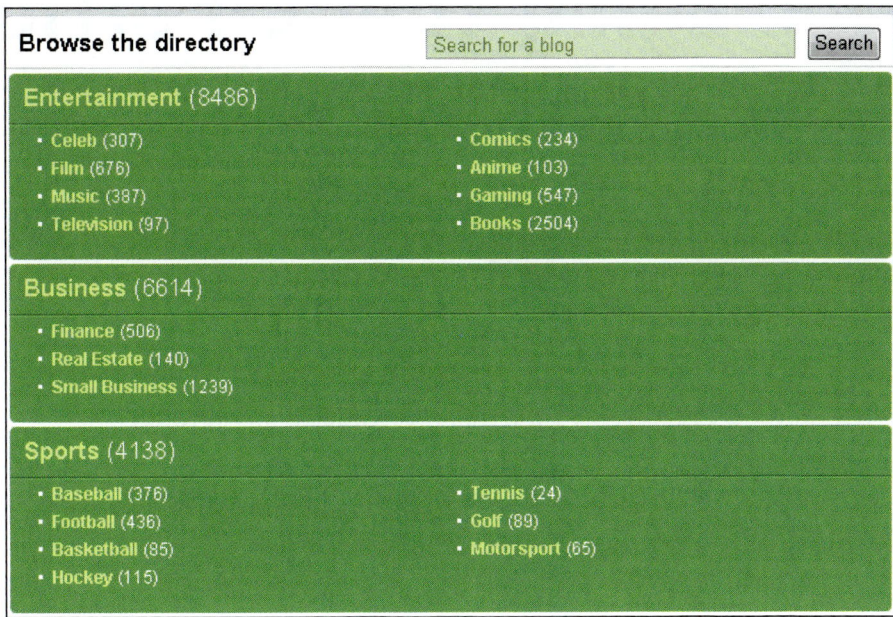

FIGURE D-13: Start a blog on WordPress

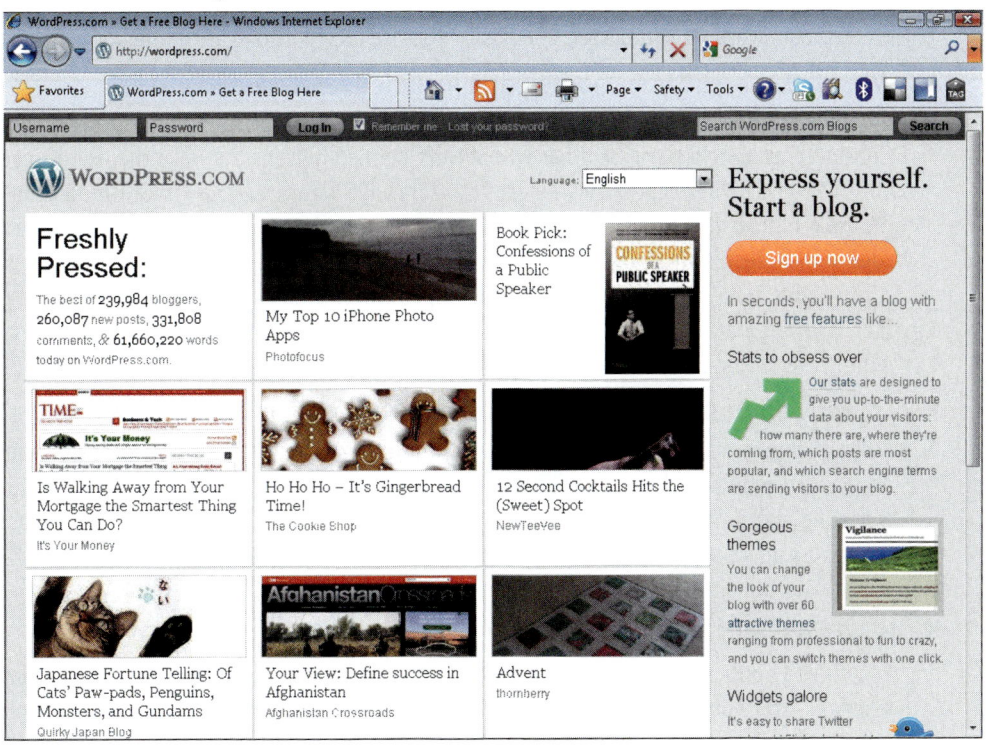

Making your blog work for you

Some blogging sites can actually earn money for you. For example, Google lets you sign up for a program called AdSense, which posts ads on your blog pages using two kinds of targeting: contextual and placement. **Contextual targeting** analyzes keywords and frequently used words in your blog to match ads to blog content. **Placement targeting** lets advertisers determine if the readers of your blog would be a match for their product. Every time a user clicks an ad from your site, you earn money. If you would prefer to have some control over which ads appear on your blog, you can use filters to block certain products, companies, or product types. *Note*: Before you sign up for a service like AdSense, you should consider your audience. Would they be pleased or annoyed by seeing ads on your blog? Also keep in mind that if your blog is school-based or institution-based, online policy might forbid you from including advertisements.

Perfecting Your Online Persona

Managing Your E-Portfolio

You have taken pains to create an e-persona that shows you in the best possible light. You belong to social and professional networks, you author a blog, and you have a following on Twitter. You have created a Web presence that will work for you even when you are offline. How can you ensure that anyone who is interested can easily put all of these pieces together? In fact, you can do it for them by creating an electronic portfolio, or e-portfolio. An **e-portfolio** is your personal home page, where you have gathered and posted links to your online information. You decide to explore which elements of your Web persona you would like to gather in a single place.

DETAILS

When putting together an e-portfolio, consider the following:

- **What will your home page look like?**

  As you have seen in your exploration of Web 2.0 tools, first impressions count for a great deal. With an e-portfolio, you can control a viewer's first impression by showcasing your strengths on the home page. If you are an artist hoping to land a job in a graphic design department, consider designing your own personal logo for the top of the page. If you are looking for a job in advertising, create and post a multimedia presentation about the product you are trying to sell: yourself. Figure D-14 shows the e-portfolio of a writer and filmmaker, who used the tools on WordPress to create the portfolio. The home page is primarily text. Figure D-15 shows the home page of the e-portfolio of a visual artist. Notice that it is dominated by samples of the artist's work. As you can see, the possibilities for an e-portfolio are limited only by your imagination.

- **What links should your home page include?**

  If you have an extensive Web presence, you will not be able to fit all of your information on a single page. Consider including a navigation bar with clearly defined buttons that take the user to pages of additional information. The navigation bar in Figure D-14 includes buttons called Links, Contact, and Clips. Clicking the Links button takes you to a list of "interesting people, places, and things" that contribute to your knowledge of who the filmmaker is. Clicking Clips takes you to her film clips and writing samples. The navigation bar in Figure D-15 includes links to the artist's paintings, exhibits, bio, press releases, and contact information. If you follow these links, you get a full portrait of the artist—and it's the portrait she has constructed by pulling everything together for you.

- **Should you post copyrighted material?**

  Posting samples of your written work, images, music, or video, is a great way to share them with the world. As you learned in Unit B, to avoid confusion, you should include the copyright status you've assigned to your work—full rights, ©, or a Creative Commons license. If you are using another person's music, photographs or other work, make sure that you have permission to use them, or that you comply with their license and terms of use.

- **How frequently should you update your portfolio?**

  You should consider updating your portfolio whenever there has been a change in your work or school situation, or if you have won an award or been given special recognition for an accomplishment. If your e-portfolio links to your blog, this information will probably be available, anyway, but if the information is significant, you'll want to showcase it up front.

Perfecting Your Online Persona

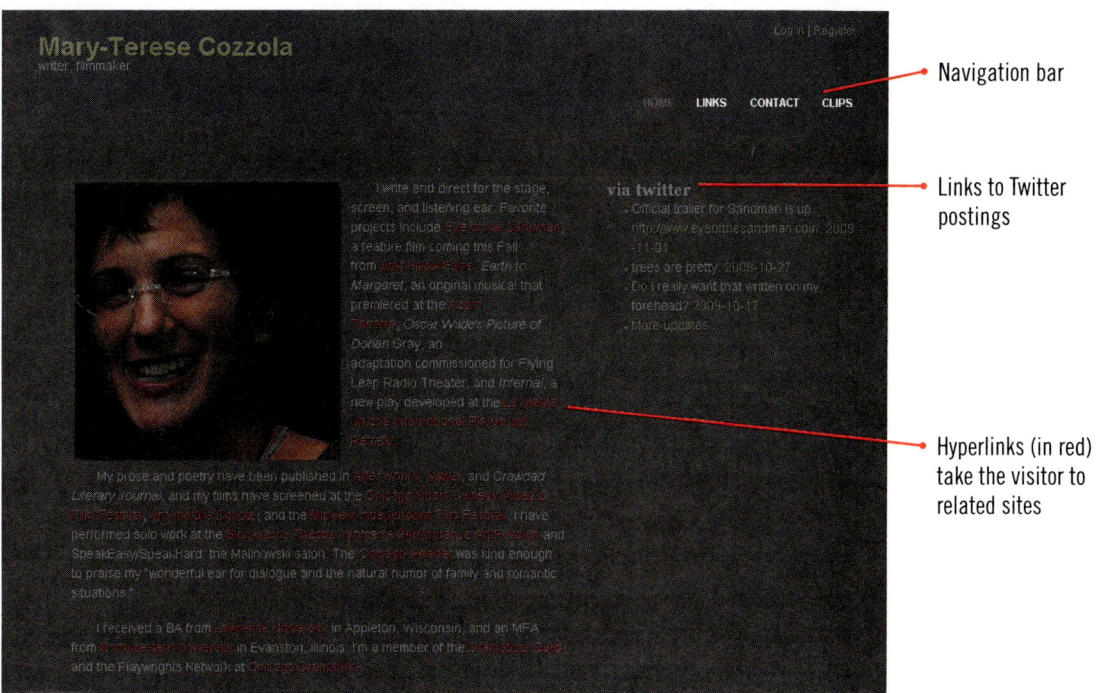

FIGURE D-14: The e-portfolio of a writer and filmmaker

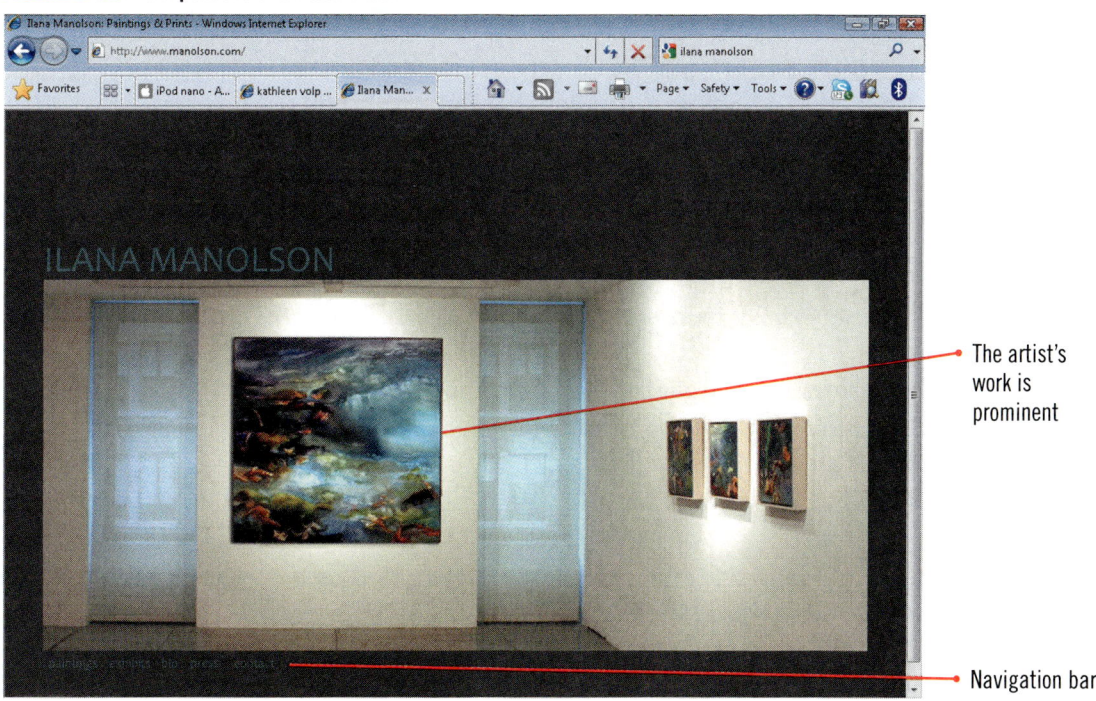

FIGURE D-15: The e-portfolio of a visual artist

Cyberstalking

One unwelcome feature of the Web is the ability to bully, stalk, or harass an individual online. **Cyberstalking** is the obsessive following of another person on the Web. In its most benign form, it involves visiting a person's profile multiple times a day, but not taking any action. Cyberstalking takes a nasty turn when the stalker starts to attack a victim using email, blogs, and networking sites with the intent of either damaging a person's reputation or intimidating that person. You will hear other terms used to describe this behavior, including **cyber bullying** when a minor is involved, and **cyber harassment**. Definitions of these terms vary, with some defining more ominous behavior (like posting threats) as stalking, and attacks on a person's character as harassment. If you are being stalked or harassed, you should know that you can protect yourself by reporting the person who is stalking or harassing you. For more information about cyberstalking, go to http://www.wiredsafety.org.

Perfecting Your Online Persona

Practice

Key Terms

background check	e-persona	mission statement	viral
contextual targeting	e-portfolio	online persona	virtual self
corporate blogger	headline	placement targeting	visibility
cyber bullying	imposter	reputation management	webinar
cyber harassment	Internet service	firm	Webmaster
cyberstalking	provider (ISP)	teleseminar	white paper
deep Web	mentor	username	

Unit Review

1. List two elements that make up your e-persona.
2. Why should you carefully consider each friend request before you accept it?
3. How can you control your visibility on a site like Facebook?
4. What is the purpose of a background check?
5. Why might it be damaging to your reputation if someone sets up an imposter account?
6. Discuss two key differences between social networking and professional networking.
7. Name three services that an online professional organization can provide.
8. What is the difference between a blog and a microblog?
9. Why might a reader object to seeing ads on your blog?
10. What is the purpose of an e-portfolio?

Fill in the best answer.

1. An employer can use Web 2.0 tools to perform a(n) _____ _____ in order to learn more about you.
2. When you join a professional organization, you might be matched up with a(n) _____ who can provide advice and help you develop important career skills.
3. Your online identity is also called your e-_____.
4. Many online organizations publish a(n) _____ _____, which defines the goals of the organization.
5. _____ _____ is a form of advertising that uses keywords from your blog or Web site to determine which ads to place there.
6. A corporate _____ contributes frequently to a log that discusses the latest products or services offered by a particular corporation.
7. Your _____ determines how easy or difficult it is to search for you on the Web.
8. A _____ is in charge of the content on a Web site, and can be contacted in case of trouble.
9. A person who sets up a fake account and pretends to be someone else is called a(n) _____.
10. A(n) _____ is the description of your position on LinkedIn.

Select the best answer from the list of choices.

1. **Who has access to your profile photo on Facebook?**
   a. Only your friends.
   b. Anyone who searches for you.
   c. Only your friends and friends of friends.
   d. Only the Facebook Webmaster.

2. **What happens when a friend on Facebook runs a Facebook application?**
   a. The application has access to all of your public information unless you have changed your Privacy Settings.
   b. The application has access to the information selected on the Applications page.
   c. The application can only access your wall.
   d. The application has access to all of your information.

3. **What kinds of information can a background check turn up?**
   a. Information that you have posted on the Web.
   b. Information posted by an imposter or by someone with the same name.
   c. Financial information that you have posted on sites that aren't secure.
   d. All of the above.

4. **What is the deep Web?**
   a. Another name for the World Wide Web.
   b. Another name for the Internet.
   c. All of the Web, including databases on social networking and other sites.
   d. Another word for a domain name.

5. **What should you do if you discover that someone is impersonating you online?**
   a. There is nothing you can do.
   b. You should contact the site and try to have the account removed.
   c. You should friend the imposter and post accusations on the wall.
   d. You should blog about the site so that everyone knows it isn't yours.

6. **What is a Google Alert?**
   a. A filter that lets you know when a Web site is a phishing site.
   b. An automated weather forecast sent to your desktop.
   c. The dialog box that appears when Google cannot find the information you have requested.
   d. An automated search feature that sends daily updates based on the keywords you supply.

7. **What is the main benefit of creating an e-portfolio?**
   a. Your employer won't be able to see how frequently you use the Web.
   b. You can save on paper and postage.
   c. You can gather your important online information in one place.
   d. Your friends can use it to post photos of you.

8. **Which of the following is associated with a microblog?**
   a. Focuses on the subject of microeconomics.
   b. Is a shortened version of one of your regular blog postings.
   c. Distills the contents of all of your blog postings into a single listing.
   d. Only allows the author to post a limited number of characters.

Independent Challenge 1

You are the administrative assistant to Sarah Pierce, the vice president of marketing at a national hotel chain. She has a short list of candidates for the job of marketing director. This person will travel the country, and will be the corporate face of the chain at sales meetings and conventions. She asks you to do an online background check of each of the applicants and present her with a report. (*Note*: You can print or post this assignment. Please check with your instructor for assignment submission instructions.)

    a. Do a background check on your name or ask a classmate or friend for permission to run an online background check on him or her.
    b. Start your research by going to pipl.com and searching on your friend's name.
    c. How many results did you get? Are they all about your friend, or do they include others with the same name?
    d. What kinds of information did the tool find? Can you rate its reliability?
    e. Print or save the results page, and then close your browser.

Independent Challenge 2

You have a work study position in the career counseling office of your college. The office would like to help students get a head start on their careers, and has asked you to compile a list of online professional organizations that have student memberships. (*Note*: You can print or post this assignment. Please check with your instructor for assignment submission instructions.)

    a. Open a new document in a word processor, then save it as **ProfessionalOrgs**.
    b. Make a table that lists three possible career paths. (*Hint*: Don't limit yourself by being too specific. For example, don't list a job title, but rather list an area, like environmental engineering or comedy writing.)
    c. Using your browser and your Web 2.0 search skills, find at least two professional organizations for each career path. (*Hint*: Do not list the professional organizations used as examples in the lessons.)
    d. In your document, list the membership options for each of the organizations, and give details about the services offered.
    e. Choose one of the organizations, and print or save its home page.
    f. Save and close ProfessionalOrgs, and then close your browser.

Independent Challenge 3

You have decided to enter the world of blogging. You are ambitious, and you want your blog to gain popularity quickly. You decide to explore the ways in which you can increase your blog visibility. (*Note*: You can print or post this assignment. Please check with your instructor for assignment submission instructions.)

    a. Go to www.wordpress.com/features and read the information on the page.
    b. Open a new document in a word processor, then save it as **WPBlogging**. Make a list of the features WordPress offers.
    c. Choose one positive feature and explain why it might help to popularize your blog.
    d. Choose one feature readers might not like and explain why. If instead you think all of the features will be valuable to your readership, explain why.
    e. Save WPBlogging, close your word processor, then close your browser.

Independent Challenge 4

You work in the public relations department of an investment firm with clients all over the world. Your company recently had to lay off 3,000 workers worldwide. Because you know how quickly news and rumors spread on the Web—especially bad news—you have decided to hire a reputation management firm to help track down any negative press your firm is getting from disgruntled former employees.

a. Use the search engine of your choice to search on the term **reputation management**.
b. Print or save the search results page.
c. Go to the Web sites of three firms that specialize in this area. (*Hint*: Not all of your search results will link to reputation management firms. Make sure that the pages you do go to provide that service.)
d. Open a new document in a word processor, then save it as **RepMan**.
e. Summarize the information you find about each of the three firms, including the company name, key services, and cost of the service.
f. Save or print the About or About Us page of one of the firms, then close the word processor and your Web browser.

Visual Workshop

Use your Web 2.0 research skills to find the Web page picture below. (*Hint*: Use Google or the search engine of your choice and look for the Boston Breakers blog.)

a. Navigate through the blog by clicking the latest blog posts.
b. What Web 2.0 tools does this blog use?
c. How is this blog organized? Does it categorize postings? Tag them?
d. Click the Privacy link at the bottom of the Web page and read the Privacy Policy. Pay particular attention to the Passive Data Collection, Third Party Advertisers, and Email Communications and Unsolicited Commercial Email sections.
e. Are there any hidden costs when you provide personal information on a Web site?

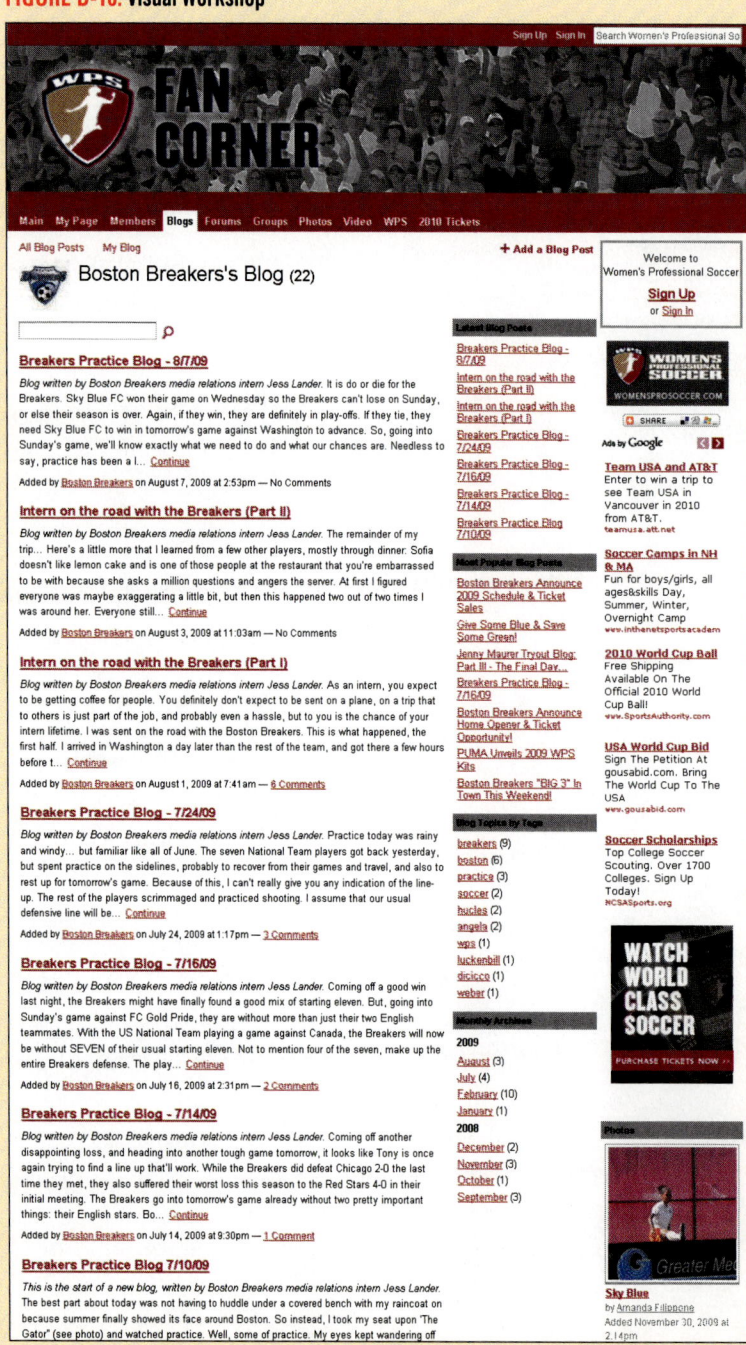

FIGURE D-16: Visual Workshop

Glossary

Action items Tasks individual members of a group agree to work on.

Agenda A list of items you plan to discuss at a meeting.

Author The creator and owner of a copyright-protected work.

Background check Research on an individual in order to determine hiring eligibility and/or general character.

Bias In a poll, a preference for one answer over another.

Bibliography A list of references cited in your work.

Blog An online journal or log updated frequently. A contraction of the words Web and log.

Bookmark A Firefox, Chrome, and Safari feature that lets you store a Web address with your browser so that you can return to it later. Also called a Favorite in Internet Explorer.

Brainstorm Generate numerous ideas on a particular topic very quickly.

Brand A product or service for sale, including the experiences the customer associates with it.

Bundle of rights The collection of legal rights granted to copyright owners.

Cite Credit a source.

Cloud computing A service where software and user files are stored on a server on the Web rather than locally on a hard drive or company server.

Contextual targeting Used by blog services to analyze keywords and frequently used words to match ads to blog content.

Conversational search engine A search service that sends updates whenever a person with standing in the industry or area of interest comments about a company or other topic online.

Copyright infringement The unauthorized use of one or more of the rights of a copyright holder.

Copyright law The legal protections granted authors of original works, whether those works are published or unpublished.

Corporate blogger A person whose role it is to present weekly updates on the latest products or technology offered by a company.

Creative Commons (CC) An alternative to traditional copyright licensing that allows copyright owners to assign the level of protection to a work.

CSV file Comma-separated-values file.

Cyber bullying Obsessively following or harassing another individual on the Web. Used most often when minors are the victims.

Cyber harassment Online actions, such as verbal attacks or intimidation directed at another individual.

Cyber stalking Obsessive following of another person on the Web, for example, attacking a victim using email, blogs, and networking sites with the intent of either damaging a person's reputation or intimidating that person.

Data mining The process of gathering consumer information and then analyzing it in order to target potential customers.

Deep Web Information contained in databases and other sites that most Internet search engines do not access.

Derivative work A new work based on an original protected work; a right granted to the copyright owner.

Digital watermark Digital data embedded into an image, audio, or video file that includes information about the copyright owner.

Direct quotation The exact words from a source you are using. Not your own work.

Domain name The full Web address of a site.

Drill down To go from a tertiary source to a primary source by clicking a series of links. Also used to describe going through a hierarchy of folders on a hard drive.

E-book A book in digital (electronic) format.

Encyclopedia A comprehensive collection of articles on different topics.

E-persona What a person "looks like" online. Includes postings by the individual, but also postings by others about an individual, public records, and news. *See* virtual self and online persona.

E-portfolio Your personal home page, where you have gathered and posted links to your online information.

Fair use A built-in limitation to copyright protection that allows users to copy all or part of a copyrighted work.

Favorite An Internet Explorer feature that lets you store a Web address with your browser so that you can return to it later. Also called a Bookmark in Firefox, Chrome, and Safari.

Follower A person who signs up to receive blog updates.

General knowledge Information that is commonly known and does not need to be credited to a particular source.

Hard copy The printed version of a magazine, book, or other publication.

Headline On LinkedIn, the main descriptor in your profile, for example, a job title.

Highlighting tools Web 2.0 tools that let you mark text on a Web page with a color to make that text stand out.

Imposter A person who sets up a social network account pretending to be another person.

Intellectual property An idea or creation that has the potential for commercial value.

Interlibrary loan program A service that lets libraries share resources.

Internet A network of computers around the world.

Internet service provider (ISP) Company that provides Internet access.

ISBN (International Standard Book Number) A unique number assigned to a publication.

Keyword A search term.

Kindle A handheld electronic reading device.

Labels Words or phrases used to tag a site so that you can return to it easily.

Mashups Mixed content from different sources that forms a derivative work.

Meeting minutes Notes from a meeting.

Mentor A person who can help guide you as you develop the skills you'll need in your career.

Metadata In digital photography, information such as camera type, exposure, shutter speed, and date.

Meta-search engine A tool that uses multiple search engines for a single search.

Microblog An extremely short blog posting.

Mind-mapping software A tool that lets you record information in a graphic format using shapes and arrows. Also called note-taking software.

Mission statement An organization's stated goals.

Model release Written permission given from a recognizable photographic subject to a photographer to use their image in a commercial work.

Nonsubscription databases A database organized by subject that does not require a fee to access.

Note-taking software A tool that lets you record information in a graphic format using shapes and arrows. Also called mind-mapping software.

Online persona What a person "looks like" online. Includes postings by the individual, but also postings by others about an individual, public records, and news. *See* virtual self and e-persona.

Paraphrase Putting an idea from your research into your own words.

Phishing filter A feature that lets you know when a Web site is suspect and might be trying to steal your information.

Photostream Photos you uploaded to an online photo-sharing service.

Placement targeting A blog service that lets advertisers determine if the readers of your blog would be a match for their product.

Plagiarism Presenting someone else's ideas and words as your own.

Podcast An audio or video file meant to be played on an iPod or other multimedia device, such as a computer or handheld device like a Blackberry.

Primary source Documents, recordings, videos, or photographs created at the time of a particular event.

Push poll A poll designed to push a respondent toward one idea or candidate and away from another.

Reputation management firm A company offering a fee-based service that helps to clean up online posts about a person and improve his or her online reputation.

Research database A collection of data or links to data in many formats, including white papers and magazine, journal, and newspaper articles.

Right of privacy Protects from interference with a common right to be left alone and to be protected from unwarranted publicity.

Right of publicity Protects against the use of an individual's likeness for commercial advantage.

Royalty The fee paid to a copyright holder for the right to use their work.

RSS feed Really Simple Syndication feed. Provides a subscriber with information from frequently updated Web content, such as podcasts, blogs, and microblogs.

Search engine A Web site that finds documents or media related to search terms or keywords that you provide.

Secondary source Discusses and analyzes the information found in primary sources.

Social bookmarks Bookmarks, or links to Web sites, that you share with friends, classmates, or with the entire Web community.

Software as a Service (SaaS) A Web service that lets you use software online and pay for it only as you use it.

Specifications Product requirements.

Streaming media Media constantly playing, received by, and normally presented to an end user while a browser delivers it.

Subject guide A search engine with information already categorized by topic.

Subscription database A collection of data or links to data in many formats, including white papers and magazine, journal, and newspaper articles that is regularly updated by its owner and requires a fee to use.

Tag cloud A type of weighted list that shows user-generated tags in different sizes based on their popularity.

Tagging A process that lets you retrieve previously visited sites using words or phrases (tags) that you assign when you create a bookmark.

Tags Words or phrases assigned to a bookmark to categorize it.

Teleseminar Recording of an online presentation available for viewing later.

Tertiary source A reference at least two steps removed from the primary source. An encyclopedia, which is the compilation of information from multiple primary and secondary sources, would be considered a tertiary source.

Thesis A summary statement of your main argument or point.

Topic sentences Statements that support your thesis.

Top-level domain (TLD) The last letters in a domain name, to the right of the period.

Tweet A posting on the microblog Twitter.

Username The name that precedes the @ sign and domain name in your email address.

Vetted Checked for accuracy by a subject matter expert.

Viral A description of online postings, photographs, and videos that travel around the world in a matter of seconds or minutes.

Virtual Existing online, such as a virtual (online) community.

Virtual self What a person "looks like" online. Includes postings by the individual, but also postings by others about an individual, public records, and news. *See* e-persona and online persona.

Virtual world Online community.

Visibility Setting that determines whether or not certain levels of users can search for you on a social networking site.

Web 2.0 technology A Web feature that gives the user the ability to collaborate with others, interact in virtual or online communities, and generate Web content.

Webinar An online seminar, sometimes recorded for later access.

Webmaster Person in charge of a Web site's contents.

White paper Informational, authoritative report.

Wiki A collaborative Web site, where users can post information and edit each other's work.

Wikipedia An online encyclopedia, edited and updated by the public.

Works cited A bibliography, or list of sources used in your research.

World Wide Web A collection of Web sites, which, in turn, are made up of multiple Web pages connected via links that a user clicks to navigate.

Index

Note: Page numbers in boldface indicate key terms.

123people.com, 72

A

action items, **52**
adding bookmarks online, 12
addresses, e-mail, 68–69
AdSense, 79
advertisement targeting, 79
agendas
    meeting, **52**
    sample (fig.), 53
Amazon Simple Storage Service (S3), 59
Amazon.com, 50–51
American Idol, 56
amplify.com, 13
animation, obtaining permissions, 34–35
APA citation format, 16
application for copyright, 40–41
art, obtaining permissions, 34–35
audio
    finding music, 32–33
    obtaining permissions, 34–35
    and online collaboration tools, 61
author, **24**

B

background checks, 72
Backtype.com, 50–51
bias, 56
bibliographies, creating, **16**–17
bibme.org, 16, 17
blogger.com, 78
blogs
    described, **48**
    writing, 78–79
    and your e-persona, 68–69
bookmarks, **12**
books vs. other sources, 7
BrainReactions.net, 54–55
brainstorming
    concepts, examples, 54–55
    described, **15**
brands, 50
bundle of rights, **24**
business, conducting from the 'clouds,' 59

C

ccMultimedia, 32
Cengage Learning, 60–61
citing sources, **16**–17
Clipmarks.com, 12, 13
cloud computing
    business and, 59
    described, **58**
Clusty, 4
collaboration tools, 2
collaborative software, using, 58–59
college graduates, advice for, 74
.com Web sites, 10
contacting authors, sources, 10
contextual targeting, **79**
conversational search engines, 50
copyright infringement, **25**
copyright law, **24**
copyrighted material, posting, 80
corporate bloggers, 78
Creative Commons (CC) licensing
    and mashups, 32
    posting files online, 38–39, 80
    using, **26**–27
crediting sources, 34–35
CSV (comma separated value), 61
CSV (comma separated value) file, 56
customer support, 50
cyber bullying, **81**
cyber harassment, **81**
cyberstalking, **81**

D

data mining, 50
databases, 4
deep Web, **72**
deleting bookmarks online, 12
Delicious.com, 13
derivative work, **24**
digital watermark, **40**–41
Dilgo.com, 13
direct quotations, **16**, 17
documentation, meeting notes, 52
domain names, 10
doodle.com, 52–53
drill down, 8

E

Eastman, George, 28
Eastman Kodak Company, 28
EasyBib, 16
e-books, 7
.edu Web sites, 8
e-mail address, and your e-persona, 68
EMOL (Entertainment Magazine Online) Web site, 36–37
encyclopedia, 6, 7, 8
e-persona
    See also online persona
    described, **68**
e-portfolio
    described, **80**
    managing your, 80–81

F

Facebook, 54–55, 68, 71
fair use
    analyzing factors of, 25
    described, **24**
    examples of, 38
favorites, **12**
files
    downloading, 30
    posting online, 38–39
film, obtaining permissions, 34–35
filters, phishing, **3**
finding
    images, 28–29
    media for your projects, 2
    music, 32–33
    primary sources, 8–9
    video, 30–31
    Web sites' terms of use, 36–37
flickr.com, 28–29, 38–39
followers, 48

G

general knowledge, **16**
Google bookmarks, 12–13
Google Calendar, 52
Google Docs, 58–59

Google Scholar, 4–5, 10
Google search engine, 4
Google Wave collaboration tool, 58
.gov Web sites, 8
government Web sites, viewing, 48–49

H

hard copy, 7
headlines (LinkedIn), 74–75
highlighting tools, 12
home page, your, 80–81
Hulu, 30

I

images
   See also photos
   finding, 28–29
   obtaining permissions, 34–35
importing local bookmarks, 12
imposters, 72
intellectual property, 24
interlibrary loan library, 4
International Association of Business Communicators (IABC), 76
Internet, 2
Internet Archives, 30–31
Internet service provider (ISP), 68
ISBN (International Standard Book Number), 7

J

jamendo.com, 33, 38–39
job postings, 76

K

keywords, 4
Kindle, 7

L

labels, 12
libraries, interlibrary loan, 4
licensing, 26–27
LinkedIn, 74–75, 76
links
   sponsored, 5
   on your home page, 80–81

M

mashups, creating, 32
media
   finding for projects, 23
   finding for your projects, 2
   streaming, 30
meeting minutes, 52

meetings
   brainstorming concepts, examples, 54–55
   scheduling, 52–53
mentors, 76
metadata, 40
meta-search engines, 4
microblogs
   described, **48**
   writing, 78–79
Microsoft Outlook's scheduling feature, 52
mind-mapping software, 2
mind-mapping tools, 14–15
mindmeister.com, 14
mission statements, 76
MLA citation format, 16
model release, 30
moderating
   meetings, 52–53
   online brainstorming session, 54–55
multimedia, obtaining permissions, 34–35
music
   finding, 32–33
   obtaining permissions, 34–35
   posting on Internet, 32
   uploading, 38
MySpace, 68, 72–73

N

NASA Web site, 10–11
NASA's CoLab, 48–49
networking, professional, 74–75
NOAA (National Oceanic and Atmospheric Administration) Web site, 36–37
nonsubscription databases, 4
notes, taking, 14–15
note-taking software, 2, 14–15

O

obtaining permissions, 34–35
online catalogs, 5
online collaboration, 58–59, 60–61
online persona
   creating your virtual self, 68–69
   described, **68**
   ensuring privacy, 70–71
   how the virtual world sees you, 72–73
   managing your e-portfolio, 80–81
   perfecting your, 67
   professional networking, organizations, 74–77
   working with blogs, microblogs, 78–79
online polling, 56–57
open access license, 26
Open Clip Library, 36–37
organizations, professional, 76–77
organizing notes, 14–15
OttoBib, 16, 17
Outlook's scheduling feature, 52
OWL Multimedia, 32

P

paraphrases, 16
peer-reviewed sources, 6
people, searching for on deep Web, 72–73
permissions
   for citations, 16
   model release, 30
   obtaining, 34–35
personal information, 70–71
phishing filters, 3
photos
   See also images
   posting, 73
   profile, 68–69
   searching for by CC license, 28
photostream, 28
pipl.com, 72–73
placement targeting, **79**
plagiarism, 16
podcasts
   described, **48**
   Prime Minister of Canada's, 48–49
polldaddy.com, 56
polleverywhere.com, 56–57
polling, conducting online, 56–57
pop-ups, blocking or temporarily allowing, 32
posting
   copyright notice on your work, 40
   copyrighted material, 80
   files online, 38–39
   information, and privacy, 70–71
   job postings, 76
   microblogs, 78
   music, 32
   photos, video, 73
Prelinger Archives, 30–31
prezi.com, 61
primary sources
   described, **6–7**
   finding, 8–9
Prime Minister of Canada's podcasts, 48–49
privacy
   ensuring your, 70–71
   right of privacy, 30
   and Web hazards, 3
professional networking, 74–75
professional organizations, choosing, 76–77
projects, finding media for, 23
protecting rights to your work, 40–41
public domain, copyright infringement and, **25**
push polls, 57

R

registering work with Copyright Office, 40–41
rehearsing presentations, 60–61
reputation management firms, **72**
requesting permissions, 34–35
research
   collaborative software, using, 58–59

finding best sources, 6–7
meetings, brainstorming, 52–55
obtaining permissions, crediting sources, 34–35
online polling, 56–57
presenting your work, 60–61
tools generally, 3–5
research databases, 5
responding to negative posts, 72–73
right of privacy, 30
right of publicity, 30
rights
copyright law, 24–25
protecting your, 40–41
roles, in presentations, 60–61
royalties, 34
RSS feeds, 48

S

saving downloaded files, 30
scheduling meetings, 52–53
search engines
conversational, **50**
described, **4–5**
SearchEdu.com, 10
Second Life, 48
secondary sources, 6–7
security
cyberstalking, bullying, harassment, 81
ensuring privacy, 70–71
and online collaboration tools, 61
posting photos, videos, 73
protecting your online persona, 68–73
of your online documents, 58–59
Sermo.com, 76–77
sharing information generally, 47
SmartBoard, 60
social bookmarks, 12
social networking
ensuring privacy on, 70–71
government use of, 48–49
and your e-persona, 68–69
software
brainstorming, 52–53
collaborative, 58–59
note-taking, 14–15
Software as a Service (SaaS), 58
sources
citing in bibliographies, 16–17
crediting, 34–35
judging validity of, 10–11
primary, secondary, tertiary, 6–9
specialized meta-search engines, 4

specifications (product requirements), 60
spokeo.com, 72
sponsored links, 5
statutory damages, 40
streaming media, 30
subject guides, 4–5
subscription databases, 4
surveymonkey.com, 56

T

tag clouds, 28
tagging, **12**
tags, **12**
taking notes, 14–15
targeting, contextual and placement, 79
telephone polling, 56
teleseminars, 76
terms of use, 36–37
tertiary sources, 6–7
text, obtaining permissions, 34–35
thesis described, 15
tools
collaboration, 2, 61
highlighting, 12
mind-mapping, 14–15
researching online personas, 72–73
topic sentences, 15
top-level domains (TLDs)
described, **10**
and meanings (table), 11
tweets
described, **48**
and your e-persona, 68–69
Twitter, 48, 68

U

University of Delaware subject guide, 4–5
updating your e-portfolio, 80
U.S. Copyright Office Web site, 24–25, 40–41
usernames, 68

V

vetted, 10
video
finding, 30–31
obtaining permissions, 34–35
and online collaboration tools, 61
posting, 73
viewing
government Web sites, 48–49
tag clouds, 28

virtual conference rooms, 2–3
virtual described, **2**
virtual self
See also online persona
described, **68**
virtual worlds, 48
visibility, 70

W

watermarks, digital, **40**
Wayback Machine, 30
Web 2.0 overview, 1–3
Web 2.0 technologies
business and, 50–51
collaborating, sharing information, 47
described, **2**
Wikipedia as example, 8
Web browsers, bookmarks and favorites, 11–12
Web cams, 61
Web pages, highlighting, 11–12
Web sites
bookmarking, 12–13
bookmarking (table), 13
.com, 10
ensuring privacy, 70–71
.gov, .edu, 8
terms of use, 36–37
viewing government, 48–49
webinars, 76
Webmaster, 72
white papers, 76
Wikipedia, 8, 9
wikis
described, **8**
government use of, 48–49
wiredsafety.com, 81
wordpress.com, 78–79
Works Cited list, 16
World Wide Web, **2**
WorldCat, 4
writer's block, breaking, 15

Y

Yelp social networking site, 50
YouTube, 30

Z

Zoho, 58–59